IT WON'T FLY
IF YOU DON'T TRY

IT WON'T FLY
IF YOU DON'T TRY

OR

HOW TO LET
YOUR CREATIVE GENIUS
TAKE FLIGHT

Richard Allen Farmer

MULTNOMAH

Portland, Oregon

Unless otherwise indicated, all Scripture references are from the Holy Bible: New International Version, copyright 1973, 1978, 1984 by the International Bible Society. Used by permission of Zondervan Bible Publishers.

Scripture references marked KJV are from the Holy Bible: Authorized King James Version.

Scripture references marked NASB are from the New American Standard Bible, copyright The Lockman Foundation 1960, 1962, 1963, 1968, 1971, 1972, 1973, 1975, 1977. Used by permission.

Edited by Steve Halliday
Cover and interior design by Bruce DeRoos

IT WON'T FLY IF YOU DON'T TRY
© 1992 by Richard Allen Farmer
Published by Multnomah Press
10209 SE Division Street
Portland, Oregon 97266

Multnomah Press is a ministry of
Multnomah School of the Bible
8435 NE Glisan Street
Portland, Oregon 97220

Printed in the United States of America.

Library of Congress Cataloging-in-Publication Data
Farmer, Richard Allen.
    It won't fly if you don't try, or, How to let your creative genius take flight / Richard Allen Farmer.
      p.   cm.
    Includes bibliographical references.
    ISBN 0-88070-419-5
    1. Creative ability. 2. Creative ability—Problems, exercises, etc. 3. Creative ability—Religious aspects—Christianity. I. Title. II. Title: How to let your creative genius take flight.
BF408.F28   1991
153.3'5—dc20   91-38339
                                                                                   CIP

92 93 94 95 96 97 98 99 00 01 - 10 9 8 7 6 5 4 3 2 1

DEDICATION

This book is, with deepest gratitude, dedicated to three women and three men.

To Rebecca Lucretia Brown English—grandmother, friend, Sweetie Pie, and giver of great hugs and pinches. You make me look forward to Sunday nights.

To Catherine Lanora Farmer Robinson—thanks for the gift of life and for your knowledge of each of your children's needs. Thank you for your presence at every turn.

To Rosemary Simmons Farmer—wife, lover, friend. Thou art the fairest of women and your consistent walk with our Lord is a refreshing model. Thanks for allowing me time to travel, write, preach, and concertize—often at your expense. May one of us walk the other to the grave.

To Russel Vanis Robinson, Sr.—you took us in and made it unnecessary to put "step" in front of father. Thank you.

To the Reverend Nathaniel Tyler-Lloyd who came to our home church when I was nine and who never left. Thanks for preaching, affirming, strengthening, and challenging me. You showed me the backside and underside of ministry and hid nothing from me. Thanks for more than thirty years of spiritual fathering.

To the memory of Reynolds Lloyd English, Sr. ("Pop")—grandfather, most missed friend, and one of my biggest fans. He gave me exposure to the best marriage I have seen (which lasted sixty-three years). Should I become a grandfather, I have been tutored by the very best.

CONTENTS

CHAPTER 1
A NEW WAY OF SEEING

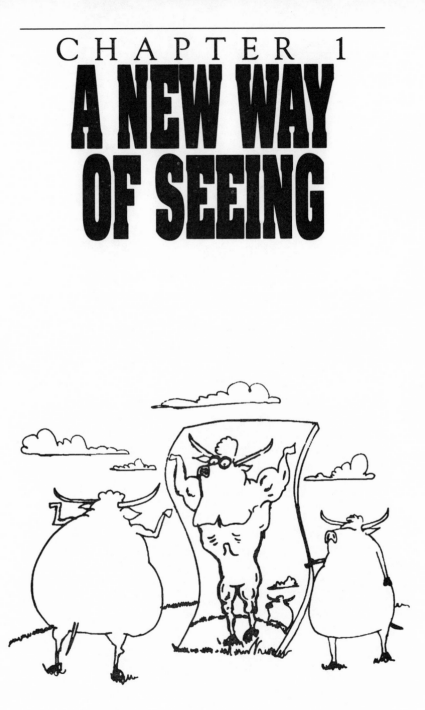

A NEW WAY OF SEEING

he room was too small for the number of participants in the workshop but we decided to make the best of it. I walked in, greeted the crowd and immediately began throwing lumps of clay into the audience. As unsuspecting "catchers" got their clay, my only instruction was "make something." As fingers went to work—kneading, bending, shaping—I began to read aloud:

This is the word that came to Jeremiah from the LORD: "Go down to the potter's house, and there I will give you my message." So I went down to the potter's house, and I saw him working at the wheel. But the pot he was shaping from the clay was marred in his hands; so the potter formed it into another pot, shaping it as it seemed best to him. Then the word of the LORD came to me: "O house of Israel, can I not do with you as this potter does?" declares the LORD. "Like clay in the hand of the potter, so are you in my hand, O house of Israel" (Jeremiah 18:1-6).

We then sang:

Have thine own way, Lord! Have thine own way!
Thou art the potter; I am the clay.
Mold me and make me after thy will;
while I am waiting, yielded and still.[1]

Because we had less than two hours allotted for our workshop, I immediately started applying what we had experienced together. Had we a larger chunk of time, we would have conducted a full-blown worship experience.

How would the average worshiper in your church react if, upon entering the sanctuary next Sunday, he or she was given a lump of clay with the simple directive, "as soon as you're seated, make something"?

Would the clay help us appreciate the Scripture reading?

Would the hymn take on new meaning?

Would the worshipers be more "focused" as they approached the varied elements of the worship experience?

The answer to this little quiz is "most likely, yes!" Given the predictable nature of most worship services, *anything* that will help us move toward freshness should be welcomed. However, we all know that too often the welcome mat is not laid out for new ideas. For many, change is threatening. One hears the words of the Gloria Patri echoing:

> As it was in the beginning
> Is now and ever shall be
> World without end,
> Amen, Amen.

When I ask participants in a workshop, "How many of you are creative?" only a few raise their hands—and even those hands are raised just enough to be seen. Rarely has a hand been raised high, with confidence.

The purpose of this book is twofold: To stimulate your creative juices by suggestion and exercise; and to get you to raise your hand high.

A NEW WAY OF SEEING

By the time we get to the epilogue, you will be comfortable raising your hand and saying, "I'm creative!" That is no more an outrageous statement than is "I was created by God." In fact, it's because you were created by a creative God and made in his image (Genesis 1:27) that *you cannot be uncreative.* Creativity is in your genes! I can hear your arguments now:

> "Others may be creative, but not me."

> "I've never been able to do anything artistic."

> "My younger sister, Gail, walked away with all the talent in our family."

> "I always wanted to be in a class for gifted children when I was in school, but I never made it."

> "Ours is a blue collar family. We were never into creative stuff."

> "I came from a small town. No museum, art galleries, symphony, or even small town band. Is it any wonder that I'm not creative?"

These arguments and others like them don't prove you're not creative. They are perceptions. You have in you the "stuff" of high creativity. Perhaps it lies dormant, but it's there. Your environment may not have encouraged it, but it's there. Your exposure to models may be scant or non-existent, but it's there.

A great sculptor was asked the details of his craft. He explained simply, "I just see a man in there and I chisel away until I get him out."

In these pages, I'm going to chisel away until I get your creative person out. This book is for the young in body and heart as well as those on whom the snowy white crown of age has been bestowed. Whether you are a worship planner, leader, office manager, rising executive, starving artist, educator, manager, domestic coordinator and engineer, fruit picker, or dog catcher, you will discover and recover your freshness—your creativity.

But before we go any further, perhaps we should ask: What is this seemingly rare commodity called creativity? Why do we need it? Let me offer a working definition of creativity for our purposes:

> *Creativity is a new way of seeing all things. It is finding angles not looked at before. It is holding an idea or problem up to the light and slowly turning it, like a multi-faceted diamond, and letting a shaft of light hit it differently each time. It is the process whereby one brings a new order out of chaos, as did our God at creation.*

A NEW WAY OF SEEING

Without this ability to see differently, life takes on a dullness, a sameness, a blandness. Before we are aware of it, we are snoring our way toward death and have not begun to tap the wondrous ideas in our minds. We need this seeing because some problems do not yield to traditional solutions. They seem to open only when probed. Those problems and their solutions remain "off limits" until we hold them up to the light.

I came at this in a non-dramatic way. I saw no flashes of thunder, no voices calling me to the creative life. I became fascinated by what I knew was an alternative to what I was seeing around me. I was driven to creativity by the lack of it. I saw people and institutions around me in a frighteningly unvaried pattern. Like a climber who has never seen his town from the summit but is sure the view is glorious, I knew there was something more.

Perhaps my being a musician helped. The arts have a way of drawing us in by their lack of concrete rules. On the piano you can do things that seem impossible. You can play the song three times, three different ways. In the arts one is invited, even encouraged, to entertain variations on a theme. I began to take an artist's view of life. I wanted to start altering the notes of life's symphony, rearrange the colors on the palette as if all of life were a painting. I wanted to push myself to try new and intricate steps as if life were a ballet.

But does this stuff work? Can I point to people and institutions made new by applying creative principles? Let me tell you about a few:

CHAPTER 1

• A now-thriving congregation in a southwestern city once wanted to build a several hundred seat sanctuary, but could not successfully raise the needed cash. Then these folks looked at the situation differently. How often would the sanctuary be used during the week? Is that what their people needed or wanted? They scrapped the plans for the worship center and built a gymnasium (which doubles as worship space) instead. They saw a dramatic increase in giving and the excitement of their people skyrocketed as they announced plans for the "sportatorium." Their gym is used seven days a week and has become a tremendous evangelistic tool as the church has reached out to the community with aerobics classes, after-school games, and instruction.

• A fast-food chain recently introduced breakfast to go as a way to grab a share of the breakfast market. It had not been getting many early morning customers, having been mostly associated with burgers and fries. Bite-sized hash browns, french toast sticks, and mini-muffins quickly increased its share of the commuter crowd.

• Corporate giant IBM loaned one of its executives to the Albany, New York, chapter of the Urban League to serve as acting president and chief executive officer. Rather than complain about the lack of civic and ethnic leadership, IBM looked at the situation differently.

• In Minnesota, educators became concerned not only about the high numbers of adolescents who were becoming parents, but also about the lack of readiness for their parenting task. Compounding the problem was the high dropout rate among teen parents, many of whom gave birth and never returned to high school. MELD (Minnesota Early Learning Design) was born to teach adolescent mothers to be better parents through talking with peers, sessions on parenting techniques from older mothers, and sharing current information on child-rearing from "facilitators." The results of this new way of seeing a problem are most encouraging. An 80 percent dropout rate has been reduced to 20 percent, while just 12 percent of those young women have a second pregnancy, down from 25 percent.

• Ben and Jerry's Ice Cream is a Vermont-based company that rewards employees for taking risks. It has instituted a Giraffe award for anyone caught sticking his or her neck out in behalf of the company. Where many companies punish risk-taking, this company encourages it. It knows there is no growth without risk, and it sees those who take risks as a company asset rather than a liability.

• Mark Victor Hansen studied with the famed inventor, Buckminster Fuller. Marketing a commercial version of Fuller's geodesic dome, Hansen was a great success. However, the skin of the domes was made with polyvinyl chloride (PVC), a petrochemical product that became scarce in the early 1970s. Almost overnight, Hansen's business became a memory. Hansen decided not to quit, but to look at his circumstances differently. What was he good at? Although his company was gone, what assets did he still have? He decided to become a professional motivational speaker, booking twenty-eight engagements in the first few weeks after he made the decision. In 1991, he had revenues of more than $2 million from speeches and tape sales.

• David H. Evans was once a salesman of ultrasonic cleaning machines. He sold these machines, which use very little water and which sterilize better than other technology, to dairies and other businesses. Inspired by drought-stricken California cities, Evans designed an ultrasonic dishwasher for restaurants and other institutions.

The common thread in each of these stories is their ordinariness. This book is written to ordinary women and men who are simply looking for another way to go at their tasks, their passions, their responsibilities, their dreams.

A NEW WAY OF SEEING

We do not have to constantly reinvent the wheel. We *are*, however, looking for new ways to *use* the wheel.

This book is written for anybody with an arsenal of old ideas who is looking for new ways to use those ideas. More than innovation (which we'll look at later), this book encourages a *new way of seeing*.

Recently I read of theCarnegie Foundation's definitions of scholarship. The report pointed out different kinds of scholarship. One kind of teaching was labeled, "synoptic capacity." It refers to a teacher's ability to "draw the strands of a field together in a way that provides both coherence and meaning, to place what is known in context and open the way for connection to be made between the knower and the known." That is what creative people do—with a passion. We take what is already known and put it in another context so that we may build a bridge between the knower, the known, and (many times) the unknown. Most people we deem highly creative may simply have a great synoptic sense. They have learned how to pull disparate parts together and come up with something else.

Rather than penalize their more curious researchers for their "noodling around," corporate giant 3M actually encourages it. The company has a "15 percent rule" which allows any employee to spend up to 15 percent of her or his work week on projects related to product development. It was that creative freedom that encouraged employee Arthur Fry, who was continually frustrated by slipping bookmarks, to perfect Post-it notes. These memo pads with very light adhesive backing have become commonplace in offices around the world and will generate millions of dollars in revenue for 3M. Most of us have faced the same problem Fry did. Fry simply saw the problem differently.

CHAPTER 1

I admire the homemaker who can think of another use for an empty frozen juice can or who thinks of a way to help her son understand and appreciate his weekly allowance. The business person who recycles an idea and uses it in the most unlikely departments or applications wins my applause. My hat goes off to the student who tackles a class project in a way unlike her peers. Her piece stands out because of her synoptic insight. It has been observed that Albert Einstein, for all his brilliance, performed no experiments and discovered no new material in order to articulate his theory of relativity. He only looked at available information differently.

By the time you complete this book you will have a different way of seeing and using existing capabilities. You need not take a course or go to a seminar for "gifted people." Through narrative and exercises, I will take some of the fear away from those who say, "I'm not creative."

Along the way, I'll give you exercises which will help you apply what I've been talking about. These T.A.B.s (**T**ake an **A**pplication **B**reak) will appear throughout the book. In fact, let's do one now.

Find an object within ten feet of where you are right now. Name the object out loud and say what it's normally used for. Now list, as rapidly as you can, ten other uses of that item in its present form. If I am in the kitchen and spot a manual can opener, I might say, "This is a can opener. It is used to open cans. It can also be used as a weapon, a book seal (by crimping the front page), a tool (for prying, banging, or digging), a hedge trimmer, an earring, a paperweight, a nutcracker, a potholder, a wrench, and a julienne potato maker."

Notice that I am not reinventing the can opener; I am thinking of other uses for it. I am seeing it differently. Much of creativity is precisely what you just did. It is taking what you already have and know and turning it around.

CHAPTER 1

Edward De Bono, one of the world's freshest thinkers in the area of creativity, likes to use the terms "lateral" and "vertical" when talking about the way we think. To think vertically is analogous to digging a hole and expanding it only by digging deeper. To think laterally is to entertain possibilities not immediately clear.

Vertical thinking is what most of us do. It is the logical, rational, straight-forward thinking with which we  were reared. When we were told to put on our thinking caps, this is the hat our teachers had in mind. Lateral thinking, however, seeks to be irrational if it must. It is not afraid to be labeled "not logical." De Bono writes in his book *New Think,*

Just as water flows down slopes, settles in hollows, and is confined to riverbeds, so vertical thinking flows along the most probable paths and by its very flow increases the probability of those paths for the future. If vertical thinking is high-probability thinking, then lateral thinking is low-probability thinking. New channels are deliberately cut to alter the flow of the water. The old channels are dammed up in the hope that the water will seek out and take to new and better patterns of flow. Sometimes the water is even sucked upwards in an unnatural fashion.

A NEW WAY OF SEEING

When the low-probability line of thought leads to an effective new idea, there is a "eureka moment," and at once the low-probability approach acquires the highest probability. It is the moment when the water sucked upward with difficulty forms a siphon and at once flows freely. This moment is the aim of lateral thinking.[2]

This book is not designed to help you dig the same hole deeper. It is designed to help you dig new holes and entertain new channels for your creative ideas.

So whether you maintain a household, manage a company, pastor a church, train sales people, or drive a cab, this book is for you.

So let's get going!

Notes

1. G. C. Stebbins, *Have Thine Own Way, Lord* (Assigned to Hope Publishing Co., 1907, Renewed 1935).

2. Edward De Bono, *New Think* (New York: Avon, 1985), 24-25.

CHAPTER 2
BEYOND "CUTE"

f we become excited about our creative capability and rise to every challenge, there is a price to be paid. At a point we may actually become counter-creative as our projects take on an absurd look. There is a great difference between being creative and being clever. One is the state out of which we bring our best ideas into being. The other is an excursion into the land of the ridiculous. Our congregations, audiences, and markets are eager for that which is creative. Nobody is waiting for us to lead them into something ridiculous. The line between creativity and ridiculousness is so thin, however, that we do not always

know when we have crossed from one to the other. We want to be creative but we don't wish to be "cute" and "clever." Consider two approaches to the same project:

Sam and Linda are the directors of the youth program at their synagogue. Knowing that they must compete with the sports program at school, the current offerings at the local theater, and the mall, Sam and Linda are constantly dreaming up new ideas. They pack their meetings with visual stimuli, changes of pace, and new experiences. On one occasion Sam and Linda wanted to teach the significance of the Law in Jewish history and culture. As far as their youth group was concerned, the Law was a dusty, irrelevant collection of teachings that stopped all fun. "How do we make it come alive?" Sam and Linda asked themselves.

When the group came to the week in which it was to discuss the commandment "Thou shalt not steal," Sam and Linda dreamed up something a little different. When the fourteen members of the group entered the meeting room, each was given $50 in cash and was told this was an anonymous gift to each person from a member of the congregation. They were then told that some games had been planned in the gym in another part of the building. "Please leave your envelopes with your money here in the room," they were told. "The room will be locked and your money will be safe."

After an exhausting hour in the gym, all returned to the meeting room. Eight people noted that their $50 were missing. Sam and Linda played dumb and shook their heads in feigned disgust as they wondered aloud who could have entered the room during the last hour. The custodian was the first suggested culprit. Sam pointed out that even if the custodian had taken the money, it was an unexpected gift and the members of the group hadn't really lost anything. "It's unfair!" was the cry.

Others in the class suggested that this is the way the cookie crumbles. Finally, after twenty minutes of losers' complaints and smug comments by those who still had their cash, Sam and Linda admitted they had orchestrated the whole event. There followed a lengthy and lively discussion about theft, offense, retribution, and general ethics. (The $50 seed money was also collected and returned to the group's treasury.) It is easy to discuss stealing when the conversationalists have not suffered a theft. But the talking takes wings when someone reports fifty dollars lifted from purse or knapsack.

Jonathan Tillman is a sales manager with Fort Nimco Travel Service. His goal is to book 20 percent more cruise passengers this year. He wants to motivate the travel agents and advertising staff to push the cruise idea whenever a client is open to a vacation suggestion. Jonathan's dilemma was how to get people thinking "cruise." He scheduled a sales meeting to present the goal.

When the agents entered, they were ushered onto a mock ship on a motorized platform where they were made seasick by violent motion for fifteen minutes while salt water was sprayed on them. After the cruise, there was a silent period of ten minutes (which seemed like an hour), to illustrate boredom. Jonathan then invited all the agents and publicists to another room that was woefully inadequate for the amount of people there.

After milling about in a cramped space for fifteen minutes, Tillman took everyone back to the first meeting room and launched into his presentation. He explained that many people have a negative view of cruises; that many travelers assume they will get seasick, bored, or be cramped in the smallest of staterooms. Tillman went on to tell his nauseated audience that they must change those perceptions.

The problem is, Jonathan has given his team a negative view, if they didn't already have one. His idea was cute and clever—but not imaginative. In fact, it was counterproductive.

CHAPTER 2

How do we know when we have crossed the line from innovation to plain weirdness?

Let me suggest some differences. Surely, no person consistently scores 100 percent in their creative planning. However, if our constituency cannot rely upon well-thought-out presentations, we will eventually lose their trust. You can pack out an auditorium solely on the weirdness and surprise for awhile, but that will not sustain a long-range business or ministry. At some point we must demonstrate that we know where the borders are. That we know the difference between prankster and pragmatist.

By the way, this is frequently a very subjective area. There's a judgment call to be made. What I consider out of place, you may find appropriate. What I consider dynamic and innovative, you may deem risky and corny. Let me, however, suggest some parameters.

That which is truly creative will not also be offensive.

Watch for paranoia here. It is possible to imagine, "All our constituents will hate this idea." Or, "The majority will vote this down." Or, "Surveys have shown our people don't want that." The reason you seek to know your audience is so that you know what you can't get away with. Don't play out your program so safely that you never stretch and test the limits.

On the other hand, don't let invisible monsters named "they" scare you. After a short period with most organizations, you will know what can work. The bottom line is, you don't want to offend values, traditions, and morals held dear by those to whom you direct your product.

I am a fan of the art of comedy. I enjoy listening to a good stand-up comedian, storyteller, or comic actress. I have noticed that there are certain topics comedians don't joke about. Even the most raunchy of them knows that they'll lose an audience if they do a string of jokes about rape, child abuse, disabled persons, or hunger.

While there are exceptions, most comics stay away from such tasteless banter. It is not that eventually they could not find a comic angle on those topics. The real problem is that we don't want to laugh out loud about such things.

People do not want to be violated on their way to creativity. To do so does not invite fresh thinking. It only causes the listener/participant to guard themselves.

Aesop has a wonderful fable in which the wind and the sun observe a man walking down a country lane. The wind tells the sun that he can make the man take off his coat faster than the sun can. They agree to compete. The wind delivers his fiercest gales but the man simply pulls his cloak more tightly around him. The sun then smiles ever so gently upon the man. With just a little more sun, the man removes his coat and whistles on his way.

We can move our people more quickly if we do not deliver offensive winds in the name of creativity. Let's bring to them the sunshine of innovation and they will, of their own accord, remove the guards and barriers and begin to think differently with us.

That which is truly creative will not also be transient.

You can ride a fad on occasion, seizing the moment because of the prevailing trend, but that's a bonus. You can't build for steady growth on that alone.

Some years ago, an innovative young man marketed a Pet Rock for those who wanted a no-maintenance pet. They sold extremely well but it was all over in a flash. That young man could not build a toy company on that idea alone. One product does not a conglomerate make. Similarly, one could not build a great sports franchise with one dynamic team. The original athletes would eventually get older and retire. The only way you can carry on is with replacement growth.

When we speak of being creative, we speak for the long term. What does this exercise do toward the fulfillment of our organizational goals? What impact will this make upon our future, be that future immediate or distant? Everything we do ought to tie into our future posture. We cannot afford to do something which doesn't help us think beyond the moment. In organizational planning, fads should not determine the agenda.

At the time of this writing, there is a form of music called Rap which is all the rage. A musical group essentially recites poetry in rhyme. A form of the protest music of the 1960s, Rap usually makes a statement about social ills, political climate, or human relationships. Some would not even call Rap a form of music because only three or four chords are used throughout the entire recitation. Like break dancing, it will pass off the scene quietly. It is not geared to be around for future generations. Neither were goldfish-swallowing contests.

Striving to be creative is the way we affirm the preselected goals of our lives or organizations. There is a purpose for the innovation. Let's revisit the illustration of the travel agent. If the goal of the agency is to give people positive travel perceptions and experiences, why not have the sales meeting on a ship? If the

Placing radio collars on animals in the wild is rather common among researchers. It allows them to track an animal's movements, migratory patterns, breedings, and life expectancy. But how do we get the view of life from the animals' perspectives? Greg Marshall, a marine biologist, has designed a video collar to be attached to large sea turtles. Pushing the idea of the radio collar a step further, Marshall can now see the turtles' responses to environment from the turtles' viewpoint. The camcorder, housed in the underwater casing, will record animal activity for two hours, either consecutively or on a time-lapse. After the predetermined recording time is expired, the camera is detached by the dissolving of critical parts of the harness. The video unit floats to the surface and data is collected. Marshall saw an existing device and then saw it differently.

stated goal of the agency is to encourage travelers to go on a cruise, it does not help to turn off the agents to that idea!

I recently read of an innovative travel agent who decided to make his office a place where you could learn about travel destinations. His agency contains a library of books on popular destinations, a video center featuring films on places of interest and several other amenities not found in your average travel agency. A traveler would be stimulated by such a place, rather than repelled by it.

If you lead a ministry that seeks to attract and train youth, then all your energies must go toward presenting biblical truth in a positive light. Even your jumping on a current, faddish bandwagon (which is not always a bad idea) must tie into the long-term goal. Transient ministry makes for transient Christians.

Essentially we have one product. We simply go at it from dozens of angles. I have never been a fan of three point, alliterative sermons. Sometimes there simply aren't three points to be gleaned from a passage of Scripture. Frequently there is only one truth, highlighted, expanded upon, and developed. If we force the passage to yield three points we have done great damage.

In our homes and businesses and ministries we run the same risk. Our business has only one goal or point. Our ministry group or organization has only one goal. Everything we do, therefore, must serve that goal. The danger of creativity, if there is one, is that we might sacrifice the eternal on the altar of the transient.

That which is truly creative will enhance the quality of life of the recipients.

Before you think I've gone too far, consider that all we offer to our constituents will either contribute to their lives or detract from them. This is not as abstract as it sounds. We, like sponges, soak in the elements of our environment if we are exposed to them long enough. If that is true, then what we offer in programming, strategy, and presentation must be carefully considered. When the aim is to be cute, clever, and wild, we do not make the kinds of changes we could make in a hearer's perception. If we would be serious about creativity, we must strategically use it to enhance and elevate our homes, congregations, sales forces, productivity teams, classes, faculty, and general constituency. I am indebted to a work by Thomas Carney for a distinction between innovation and creativity.

CHAPTER 2

Innovation is a much abused word. It has been used as a synonym for creativity, for imagination, for invention. Creative acts are innovative, but all innovation is not creative. Whenever something is done for the first time it is an innovation. When a company changes the form of an existing product it is an innovation. The introduction of spray cans to produce aerosols of products was an innovation. The replacement of aerosols by manual pumps was an innovation. King-sized cigarettes and waterbeds were innovations, and were important commercially. But they are not the kind of creative changes that are necessary for a people to assume world leadership in commerce and industry, and they are not the kinds of innovations that result in better quality of life for a nation's individuals.[1]

When we speak of creativity, we are not speaking of putting new paint on an old engine. We are, rather, intent upon a new configuration altogether. Dreaming up kooky ideas is not creativity. Being weird for the sake of being weird is not creativity. To be creative is to see differently and to apply that new seeing to the predetermined goals of the environment in which you find yourself.

While he was the president of Columbia University in New York City, Dwight D. Eisenhower purchased a farm in Gettysburg, Pennsylvania. He writes: "This was a chance, I thought, to prove that careful husbandry could restore land to its original fertility. . . . Although we haven't achieved the greatest success . . . there are enough lush fields to assure me that I shall leave the place better than I found it."[2] In creative planning that is precisely what we do: we take a project or problem and we leave the situation in better shape than the way we found it. We do that without offense, without making an idol of the prevailing trend or fad, and with a goal of enriching our recipients and constituency.

The question that must be upon the lips of the creative planner is, "What difference will this make in the lives of the recipients?" Obviously that can be taken to an extreme wherein one feels obligated to justify every change of format or schedule. Each business meeting gets more dull and you have decided to freshen it up a bit. I don't know that you need to defend the use of color charts instead of the usual distribution of sheaves of paper. You might pause in your planning, however, and ask, "Would it enhance communication and comprehension if I were to show the facts graphically?" If the answer is yes, you will cut down on the ignorance in the room with your charts. You will minimize the fog that hangs over the project.

Have you ever been to an annual congregational meeting? Many parishioners have no dealings with budgets of any size. They walk into the church meeting and are expected to act on a budget of $500,000. What can you do to help them? If your aim is to wow them but not to lift them, you have failed. In your creative, idea-generating moments, have their welfare uppermost in your mind. When my presentation is over, those who have listened to me ought not only to feel better, but be better equipped to make better decisions.

Jot down three of the recent activities that you branded "creative." Analyze them. What struck you as a new way of seeing? What was fresh and different about that activity? You know you liked it, but why? Was there one angle on that event/activity that turned it around for you? If so, name it. After you have dissected three activities, isolate the creative elements and put them in a separate list. That list becomes a part of your creativity file. They are some of the items you look for in a highly creative setting. Could you implement any of those elements in your next meeting, project, or report?

BEYOND CUTE

All my life I have lived in or near major urban centers. Part of that joy is the experience of driving one's car into craters playfully called potholes, some of which have been large enough to swallow a compact car. There are two and only two ways to fix a pothole. The more common way is to pull up to the site in a truck full of asphalt. After shutting down one lane of traffic, you heat the asphalt, shovel a less-than-adequate amount into the hole, pack it tightly (reminiscent of what a dentist does with the filling in your tooth while it's still soft), turn the flashers off on your truck, and move on to the next canyon.

While the second method is more inconvenient, it is far more satisfactory in the long run. The second method involves shutting down the same lane or perhaps the whole street. With jackhammers and other noise-makers, workers strip the street down to its initial layer. They then repave the street from the bottom up. The "new" street is now good for several more years (unless, of course, we're speaking of New York City, in which case the street will be pothole-free for approximately 17.3 minutes).

When we plan, we have the opportunity to patch a hole or make a statement of lasting value. If we buy into "cute" we rarely make pronouncements that endure. If we take the time to craft a statement, draw a plan, build a model, design a chart, draft a proposal, solicit an opinion, encourage a vision, or dream a dream, we may discover that we have transcended the trend and made an impact. In creative thinking, we dare not look only at the present process but at the end result. Those who are consumed with being "relevant" at the expense of long-term effectiveness pay a great price for their consumption. The goal is diversity, not deviance. In ministry, we are always building somethings and someones. We are building a body of believers, an assembly, a congregation, an organization.

We are building saints, strong men, capable women, unswerving youth, confident children, sweet seniors, and everything in between. Those things and people must ever be in our minds lest we forget why we do what we do.

The difference between cute and creative/innovative is much like the difference between polyester and 100 percent wool. I may buy a suit of the former and enjoy it for a season. I may buy the latter and wear it for years.

Leisure suits whose only selling feature   is "they are machine washable and they don't wrinkle" do not enhance the wardrobe for very long.

If you stock your thinking closet with creative ideas, you will be sought-after for years to come. If you are known for fads and cheap thrills which last for a week, your days are numbered.

As for me and my house . . . good bye, polyester!

Notes

    1. Thomas P. Carney, *False Profits* (Notre Dame: The University of Notre Dame Press, 1981), 100.

    2. Dwight Eisenhower, *At Ease* (Blue Ridge Summit, Penn.: TAB Books, 1988), 193-194.

CHAPTER 3
THE KINGDOM IS LIKE

On a recent flight I sat in front of two women in their twenties. One was speaking of her boyfriend, who was spending most of his spare time working on an old house, remodeling it for resale. It was easy to get every word of the conversation, for these ladies spoke freely and loudly.

"He, like, works on that house every day. He's getting so tired of it."

"Is he planning to, like, live in it?"

"No, he's gonna sell it, like for a profit when he's done. I did get him to take a couple of days off and go to, like, Martha's Vineyard."

"Is that nice? I've never been there."

"Oh, it's like, so-o-o-o-o-o nice. There are, like, no hotels. They just have, like, guest houses and bungalows. It's, like, so pretty."

By the time these dazzling conversationalists softened their voices, I was not sure I remembered the true definition of the word *like*. That wonderful word of comparisons invites us to observe similarities between one truth, object, or idea and another. Often we get so bogged down with definitions that we need help in seeing the concept another way. That's where "like" legitimately comes in. A brief survey of the Old and New Testaments will yield much fruit as we, like, look for comparisons.

To the Israelites the glory of the LORD looked

like a consuming fire on top of the mountain (Exodus 24:17).

Did you not pour me out like milk and curdle me like cheese? (Job 10:10).

They grope in darkness with no light; he makes them stagger like drunkards (Job 12:25).

May born of woman is of few days and full of trouble. He springs up like a flower and withers away; like a fleeting shadow, he does not endure (Job 14:1-2).

Inside I am like bottled-up wine, like new wine-skins ready to burst (Job 32:19).

A word aptly spoken is like apples of gold in settings of silver (Proverbs 25:11).

Like a bad tooth or a lame foot is reliance on the unfaithful in times of trouble (Proverbs 25:19).

Like one who seizes a dog by the ears is a passer-by who meddles in a quarrel not his own (Proverbs 26:17).

She is like the merchant ships, bringing her food from afar (Proverbs 31:14).

His cheeks are like beds of spice yielding perfume. His lips are like lilies dripping with myrrh (Song of Songs 5:13).

Your breasts are like two fawns, twins of a gazelle. Your neck is like an ivory tower (Song of Songs 7:3-4).

But if I say, "I will not mention him or speak any more in his name," his word is in my heart like a fire, a fire shut up in my bones (Jeremiah 20:9).

As soon as Jesus was baptized, he went up out of the water. At that moment heaven was opened, and he saw the Spirit of God descending like a dove and lighting on him (Matthew 3:16).

To what can I compare this generation? They are like children sitting in the marketplaces and calling out to others (Matthew 11:16).

The kingdom of heaven is like a mustard seed, which a man took and planted in his field (Matthew 13:31).

The kingdom of heaven is like yeast that a woman took and mixed into a large amount of flour until it worked all through the dough (Matthew 13:33).

The kingdom of heaven is like treasure hidden in a field (Matthew 13:44).

CHAPTER 3

The kingdom of heaven is like a merchant looking for fine pearls (Matthew 13:45).

The kingdom of heaven is like a net that was let down into the lake and caught all kinds of fish (Matthew 13:47).

Woe to you, teachers of the law and Pharisees, you hypocrites! You are like whitewashed tombs, which look beautiful on the outside but on the inside are full of dead men's bones and everything unclean (Matthew 23:27).

I will show you what he is like who comes to me and hears my words and puts them into practice. He is like a man building a house, who dug down deep and laid the foundation on rock. . . . But the one who hears my words and does not put them into practice is like a man who built a house on the ground without a foundation (Luke 6:47-49).

What is the purpose of all this metaphor and analogy? Why can't the writers and speakers simply say what they mean? Are we so dense that we could not grasp the meaning of a given phrase without a word picture? Aren't these comparisons nothing more than mental training wheels for those who cannot think clearly? Surely we'll come to a point at which this "help" will no longer be needed.

If that is your thinking, you have missed the whole point of metaphor. The function of analogy, comparison, word pictures, and similes is to give us another way of seeing an old truth. The picture opens new possibilities to the thinker.

To take full advantage of this, you should push the analogy until it breaks down, then apply the gleanings from it to your problem. Let's look at Psalm 1 and milk the metaphor.

> Blessed is the man who does not walk in the counsel of the wicked or stand in the way of sinners or sit in the seat of mockers. But his delight is in the law of the LORD, and on his law he meditates day and night. He is like a tree planted by streams of water, which yields its fruit in season and whose leaf does not wither. Whatever he does prospers. Not so the wicked! They are like chaff that the wind blows away. Therefore the wicked will not stand in the judgment, nor sinners in the assembly of the righteous. For the LORD watches over the way of the righteous, but the way of the wicked will perish.

Let's analyze the analogy: What is there about a tree planted by streams of water that make it a suitable metaphor for righteous women and men?

Here's where you must play, open up, let loose:

1. Trees that are planted have roots.
2. Trees that are planted have trunks.
3. Trees that are planted have bark.
4. Trees that are planted by streams of water do not have the same need of nutrients that trees planted in the desert would have.

5. Trees planted by streams of water will probably produce a better crop than their arid counterparts.

Conclusions?

1. Righteous people are not to be as shaky and unreliable as the wicked, but are to be marked by their dependability and "rootedness."

2. Righteous people can be leaned upon, as one would lean upon a tree trunk.

3. Righteous people have tough, thick skins. They can withstand any adversity. They have an outer armor, like a tree trunk, that protects them from deep wounds.

4. Righteous people do not need much attention in the area of spiritual growth. They are sustained by the water of discipline that runs steadily beneath their lives.

5. Stable, righteous people will always serve and please God and exhibit more of his character (bear more fruit) than will an unstable, wicked person.

What is there about chaff that makes it an appropriate word picture for the wicked?

1. Chaff blows away if you don't capture it.

2. The wind has a plan for the chaff, if the farmer doesn't.

3. Chaff is degradable and will die.

Conclusions?

1. Wicked people will have an undesirable destiny if they are not "captured" by the righteous.

2. The forces of evil have a plan for wicked persons if the righteous reapers do not.

3. Wicked persons will die like chaff if they are not given an opportunity to become righteous.

Now, you may or may not agree with the views or

conclusions just presented. What is critical is that you learn what to do with a word picture. I always look to milk the metaphor and analyze the analogy. Perhaps you have just realized why the productivity is down in your department. Maybe you just figured out why some people in your class are growing and others are not. The ideas come as you think about the tree by the stream.

Of course, you may carry the theme of the tree and the chaff right into your solution:

> Beginning on the twenty-third of this month, we will be sponsoring a three-week course titled "Deepening Your Roots."

> Our new time management seminar, "A More Fruitful Day," will be held on Saturday, June 9.

To those lagging behind in submitting reports or sales quotas, you might say, "Don't let the wind carry your clients away. Seize every opportunity!"

Where did you get that wind idea? From ruminating on the psalm. As you spend time with this and other exercises, you will polish your ability to think differently. Analogies open yet another door so that we may get at our task. Our goal is to keep broadening our option base.

Before we move on, let me issue one caution. Realize that you can take analogy and metaphor too far. There are some limits as we extract truth from these word pictures. Often a fine picture becomes an absurd caricature in the hands of a sloppy interpreter. Be bold but careful, lest your comparison suggests poor scholarship, faulty logic, heretical theology, outdated management principles, or unrealistic thinking.

Some metaphors do not work at all. That is, you cannot do much with them except to appreciate them for their sense of poetry. Don't strain or force a meaning out of a picture when it will not yield such meaning easily. Rush in, get the gold, and run out. If you must dig and dig and dig, you probably haven't got a good one.

Generate five metaphors for worship. Going to worship services is like:

1.

2.

3.

4.

5.

Now unpack the metaphor. What is there about what you just generated that could inform the way your worship is planned, conducted, or evaluated?

CHAPTER 3

In a recent creativity workshop, I asked a group to give me, in grocery list fashion, some metaphors for worship. They began to call out:

"Worship is like going to a birthday party."

"Worship is like an oasis in the desert."

"Worship is like an embrace."

"A worship service is like a hospital."

We found it stimulating to take some of these and milk the metaphors. We worked with the image until we extracted from it those elements that would freshen our worship. For instance, what is there about a hospital that could help us plan more effective worship? All hospitals have facilities for those who are broken and needy. The emergency room is for those who have pressing needs. Does our worship or our worshiping congregation have a mechanism to take care of those who come in with dire needs? Maybe the hospital imagery will cause us to think about starting a group whose primary responsibility will be the care of spiritual "emergency cases." Every hospital has an ambulance, because it knows that sick people cannot or will not always bring themselves in. Does this make you think about the transportation needs of your congregation or company? On and on we could go, but you get the point.

Did you ever think of calling your annual missions emphasis a festival? All the world loves a festival, while few love a conference, conclave, workshop, seminar, strategy session, or assembly. Frequently a mere name change, spurred on by a metaphor, gives a fresh and more marketable standing to your project.

When I was growing up in a Baptist church in the

Bronx, we used to sing:

> Life is like a mountain railroad
> With an engineer that's brave
> We must make the run successful
> From the cradle to the grave.
> Watch the curves, the fills, the tunnels
> Never falter, never fail
> Keep your hand upon the throttle
> And your eye upon the rail.
>
> You will roll up grades of trial
> You will cross the bridge of strife
> See that Christ is your conductor
> On this lightning train of life.
> Always mindful of obstruction
> Do your duty, never fail
> Keep your hand upon the throttle
> And your eye upon the rail.
>
> You will often find obstructions
> Look for storms of wind and rain
> On a fill, a curve or trestle
> They will almost ditch your train
> Put your trust alone in Jesus
> Never falter, never fail
> Keep your hand upon the throttle
> And your eye upon the rail.
>
> As you roll across the trestle
> Spanning Jordan's swelling tide
> You behold the Union Depot
> Into which your train will glide

CHAPTER 3

Then you'll meet the Sup'rintendent
God the Father, God the Son
With the hearty, joyous plaudit,
"Weary pilgrim, welcome home."[1]

Have you thought of life using the railroad metaphor? Let's switch metaphors and see life as a bike ride. Recently a missionary couple with whom I correspond sent a newsletter that contained the following anonymous poem:

At first I saw God as my observer, my judge,
keeping track of the things I did wrong,
so as to know whether I merited heaven or hell
    when I die.
He was out there sort of like a president.
I recognized his picture when I saw it,
but I didn't really know him.

But later on when I met Christ,
it seemed as though life were rather like a bike
    ride,
but it was a tandem bike and I noticed that
    Christ
was in the back helping me pedal.

I don't know just when it was
that He suggested we change places,
but life hasn't been the same since.
When I had control
I knew the way.
It was rather boring, but predictable . . .
It was the shortest distance between two points.

THE KINGDOM IS LIKE

But when He took the lead, He knew delightful
    long cuts, up mountains and through rock
    places
at breakneck speeds.
It was all I could do to hang on!
Even though it looked like madness,
He said, "Pedal!"

I worried and was anxious and asked,
"Where are you taking me?"
He laughed and didn't answer,
and I started to learn to trust.

I forgot my boring life and entered into the
    adventure.
And when I'd say, "I'm scared,"
He'd lean back and touch my hand.

He took me to people with gifts that I needed.
Gifts of healing, acceptance, and joy.
They gave me gifts to take on my journey,
my Lord's and mine.

And we were off again.
He said, "Give the gifts away; they're extra bag-
    gage,
too much weight."
So I did . . . to the people we met.
And I found that in giving I received,
and still our burden was light.
I did not trust Him, at first, in control of my life.
I thought He'd wreck it;
but He knows bike secrets,

knows how to make it bend to take sharp cor-
ners,
knows how to jump to clear high rocks,
knows how to fly to shorten scary passages.

And I am learning to shut up and pedal in the
strangest places,
and I'm beginning to enjoy the view and the
cool breeze on my face
with my delightful, constant companion, Jesus
Christ.
And when I'm sure I just can't do anymore,
He just smiles and says . . . "Pedal!"

If you desire some fresh thinking about your company
or ministry, find a metaphor and pull truth out of it. A
word of caution: No analogy walks on all fours indefinitely.
By that I mean that even the best of metaphors will break
down eventually. Extract what you can and leave the
skeleton for another time.

List five functions you must attend in the average year (or month). Rename them, finding an analogy that compels you to see the function differently.

Example: Board meeting.

New name: Tuesday Think Tank.

See how it's done? Now you try:

Old Name   New Name

1.

2.

3.

4.

5.

CHAPTER 3

Without analogies and metaphors we can still think creatively. With analogies, however, new vistas are opened for such thinking. After Jesus told a parable on one occasion, Mark notes: "And with many such parables He was speaking the word to them as they were able to hear it; and He did not speak to them without a parable; but He was explaining everything privately to His own disciples" (Mark 4:33-34, NASB).

Translated, that simply means that Jesus the Christ, the greatest communicator of all time, frequently used word pictures. He knew that we would not always catch the subtleties and the nuances of plain speech. He knew that his followers then and now would have trouble without an analogy. For Jesus to say "it is like" is for him to make clear that he wants us to get it.

When I was a teenager, I would make a game of counting how many times my dad would say the same thing. What made the game fun was that I had to listen closely because he would not merely repeat a statement. First he would lay out the statement. Then he'd say, "In other words," and give it another shot. Then would come an illustration from the archives of his Quincy, Illinois, boyhood file. "So, what I mean is . . ." would follow and the conversation might come to an end. I am reminded of my dad when I read the fifteenth chapter of Luke. Jesus has been attracting all sorts of people as he has been teaching and preaching. According to the Pharisees (the upper crust of that day's society), Jesus has been drawing the wrong kinds. Luke simply records that "the Pharisees and the teachers of the law muttered, 'This man welcomes sinners and eats with them' " (Luke 15:2). Immediately following this charge, Jesus told three parables. He tells them in succession, without a break (or so it seems).

In the parables of the lost sheep, the lost coin, and the lost (prodigal) son, one can hear Jesus saying, "In other words." Lest the critics don't get the point of Jesus' love for lost people from his story of the lost sheep, Jesus seems to say, "Let's try another word picture. I diligently go after these sinners as one might diligently search for a lost coin." The critics might still be scratching their heads and stroking their beards. Do you see Jesus saying, "All right. Let's try another way of looking at it. My commitment to these 'undesirables' is like a father's commitment to his wayward son"? Jesus uttered but one main truth in Luke 15. He kept switching metaphors until he thought the point was made.

CHAPTER 3

The great danger of any innovator is to rely too heavily on metaphor, analogy, simile, and illustration. Avoid the temptation to turn your presentation into a story sandwich, in which you pile one anecdote upon another. What will speak well of your creative approach to your work and life is your judicious use of pictures that breathe life into a concept or project.

About ten years ago a friend of mine delivered a sermon to a group of people gathered in the middle of the week. He spoke about the "black hole" and how it reminded him of suffering. He said going through trials was like being sucked into a deep, dark abyss. Recently, he and I were visiting a woman who heard that sermon a decade earlier. She expressed thanks to him, as she has thought of the "black hole" of suffering many times since then. What a tribute to the power of comparison! Had he spoken simply of "trusting God even when you cannot figure him out," it would have been a good sermon, but probably not a

Like whoa!

memorable one. But the "black hole" image stuck in the mind of a listener for ten years!

Don't waste the word *like* in banal conversation. Save it for those times when you need to build a bridge between what is and what you long to see. Save *like* for those times when your idea won't take wing unless you change the atmosphere in which it flies. I am reluctant to give guarantees, but I can assure you that you will see a significant increase in your ability to generate fresh ideas if you will find the analogies and develop them.

If that does not work, like, write to me and I'll, like, give you a refund.

Note

1. Charlie D. Tillman, "Life's Railway to Heaven," copyright 1891. Reprinted in *The Baptist Standard Hymnal*, A. M. Townsend, ed. (Nashville: Sunday School Publishing Board).

CHAPTER 4
THE POWER OF PLAY

THE POWER OF PLAY

I t is so-o-o-o-o-o therapeutic, so life-changing, so healthy, so joy-producing . . . but so maligned. It is play—the arch-enemy of the workaholic, the guilt-producing activity of the would-be-balanced person. Yes, play—the thing you do when you're bored or you want to be deliberately non-productive. Play—that thing children do when they are not eating, sleeping, going to school, or asking why the sky is blue.

I cast my vote in favor of play. It has kept me sane and has been one of those life-saving devices that keeps me from taking my own press releases too seriously. At a Bible conference one summer, I was asked to sit on a panel with several other pastors. We were each asked to respond to the question, "What are you doing to stay fresh in ministry?"  Typical answers were, "Trying to see that I have a consistent quiet time," "Spending more time with my wife," and, "Subscribing to an aggressive reading program." Not so with my answer. "I'm learning to play more!" I blurted out. It wasn't a very "spiritual" answer but it was true.

CHAPTER 4

The person who would be authentically creative must not despise the power of play. In our fun we see parts of ourselves we do not normally see; we get a different perspective on an old problem. We grab hold of images to which we would not otherwise have access. From Old Testament times onward, play has received a less-than-good report. Do you remember what was written of Israel? It was not very complimentary:

> When the people saw that Moses was so long in coming down from the mountain, they gathered around Aaron and said, "Come, make us gods who will go before us. As for this fellow Moses who brought us up out of Egypt, we don't know what has happened to him." Aaron answered them, "Take off the gold earrings that your wives, your sons and your daughters are wearing, and bring them to me." So all the people took off their earrings and brought them to Aaron. He took what they handed him and made it into an idol cast in the shape of a calf, fashioning it with a tool. Then they said, "These are your gods, O Israel, who brought you up out of Egypt." When Aaron saw this he built an altar in front of the calf and announced, "Tomorrow there will be a festival to the LORD." So the next day the people rose early and sacrificed burnt offerings, and presented fellowship offerings. Afterward they sat down to eat and drink and got up to indulge in revelry (Exodus 32:1-6).

The King James version of Exodus 32:6 puts it, "and the people sat down to eat and to drink, and rose up to play." The New International Version more accurately translates this verse and its New Testament quotation (1 Corinthians 10:7) as, "Afterward they sat down to eat and drink and got up to indulge in [pagan] revelry." While the word "play" is not used in the NIV, the passage clearly assumes a lack of seriousness on Israel's part. To play is to be frivolous and unstructured. Whereas that may be a disadvantage for Israel, who was called to soberly, seriously demonstrate God's character to watching nations, it is an advantage for those of us who need a new way of seeing. Israel did not "play" as we know play and it certainly did not take God as seriously as he ought be taken. Therein lies the indictment.

Both the KJV and the NIV give us a picture of a people who treasured their post-worship more than their time with the living God who called them to himself. Verses 9-10 go on to show God's judgment against these play-filled worshipers.

But before we start thinking God doesn't approve of play, let's look at the context. These are the people who were formed for God's own pleasure; for his glory; for his purposes; as a visible demonstration of what a people would look like if they were completely yielded to the living God. For that plan to be implemented, Israel had to be as intentional as God was. The offense of idolatry was that for all the minutes Israel danced around that golden calf, Israel was also stating a change of allegiance . . . even if but for a moment. One gets the impression that when Israel was called to offer a sacrifice to the Lord, the people wanted to get it over with as quickly as possible and then get on with the partying.

It reminds me of worshipers on a given Sunday morning who don't mind hearing from God—provided he address them in one hour. After all, we must get on with our lives! God was eager to see Israel make some distinction between play and worship. This passage does not serve to show the inappropriateness of play. Rather, it states that Israel wallowed in revelry. They were more intent on satisfying their carnal urges than in being faithful to the God who delivered them from Egypt. They squeezed a little worship into the play time.

The play I'm talking about here does not resemble in the least the kind of play Israel practiced in the desert. The play under consideration here is critical to the creative process. Rather than argue for a seriousness that would be counter-productive, let me simply lead you in some thinking about play. There are a few problems we need to address immediately.

In our society, play does not have honor.

If you work and work hard, you are congratulated. If you work two jobs, you are admired for being industrious. If you work three jobs, you don't even have time to read this book so I won't mention those types. We are a nation of hard-working, proud-of-it people who know little about playing. Even our recreation has a warped sense of structure and order to it.

Think about the average family's vacation. We must check in at the hotel by a certain time or (unless we've prearranged a late arrival) our room may be given away.

THE POWER OF PLAY

At 9:00 A.M. we board the bus and head for the museum. At 11:30 we must reboard the bus and get to the restaurant where our tables are waiting. It is inconvenient for the eatery to hold a room for thirty of us, so we dare not arrive a minute past noon. Wolf that salad down because we're due at the Mount of Exhaustion by 2:00 P.M. where we will see a film on ancient basket weaving, followed by a tour of the ruins of the straw factory.

When I am on vacation I insist upon as little structure as possible. I want a rhythm that is radically different from my routine at home. I want to play! It seems something for which we must apologize or must flash a logbook which proves that we have worked hard enough to have "earned" the luxury of doing nothing.

"Do you work?" we ask the young mother. She must list the household tasks and make them sound arduous before she is excused or validated. Suppose she spent a significant part of her day playing with the toddlers? Most of us would not count that as "real" work. Yet, it is the play time that strengthens the motor skills of the child. It is often in the playground that cooperation and sharing are learned. Self-esteem is built as one learns to skillfully play a game or run in a certain way. As we go about building a creativity-friendly environment, we must become advocates of play. For your next board or committee meeting, plan a few minutes of games at the beginning of the meeting. A good opener might be some Symbol Simons, pictures that suggest a well-known phrase. Here are a few:

timing tim ing	0 MD BA PhD	$\dfrac{\text{EZ}}{\text{iii}}$

(Split-second timing)   (Three degrees below zero)   (Easy on the eyes)

After you insist that each board or committee member work on these for five minutes, you will have to deal with the second problem with play.

The direct benefits of play are not readily seen or experienced.

If I buy a toothpaste that promises to make my teeth whiter, I want those bicuspids and molars gleaming by the end of the first day of use. That is my right as an American—instant results! But it is not so with play. Its benefits are often subtle. For the hypersensitive, regular recreation may lower the blood pressure, but that may not be noticeable at the end of the first game of backgammon.

The games played by a committee may identify the way an individual member thinks, may uncover another's

sense of humor, or may point out an embarrassing lack on another's part. None of these observations is guaranteed to surface at the first meeting. However, over a period of time, some significant patterns and insights emerge.

Much has been written on the theory of play. The recurring question has to do with why we play. What purpose does it serve? One suggestion is that we play to burn off excess energy. We take in so much data and are exposed to so much stimuli, that from time to time we need to release it. This does not serve as a conclusive

Dan and Don Wilson market an expensive golf simulator. Their father observed that golf was gaining such popularity in the United States, that avid players would soon wish to play indoors. After much research, the Wilson brothers developed a device that allows a golfer to hit a ball into a nine-by-twelve-foot screen which projects footage of several different world famous golf courses. Their simulators are a big hit on cruise ships containing cooped-up golfers eager to swing a club and measure a drive. Many golfers have simply gone indoors when winter came, only to vicariously play, by watching television. The Wilson brothers saw the golfers' plight but saw it differently.

explanation and you can see the holes in such an explanation already, can't you?

A person enjoying play will play past a point of release to the point of exhaustion. A person who has virtually no energy will still play. His play may be, of necessity, limited and sedentary, but he will play with a sense of compulsion, not merely to get rid of excess energy.

Another theory states that play is an instinct through which we learn needed life skills. Our play serves as a rehearsal for the "real world." This theory would say that it is not only cute to see a kitten "attack" a ball of yarn, but that the kitten learns to pounce upon mice by such play. The youngsters playing with dolls learn the basics of caring for another "person." The ones playing "doctor" learn about the intricacies of the human body. Perhaps hide-and-seek was the early game of would-be bounty hunters. Maybe the game of tag was the way those who lived on freshly-caught meat learned their craft.

Some have observed that play fulfills the desire of some to have at least one area in which they are dominant. In some games the only rules you have are the ones you invent. If one plays solitaire, one need not hear another's charge of "that's not fair." In some games we answer to no one. Imagine a person who in ordinary work and life is subservient to another. That person does not get to bend rules, shape policy, determine course of action, or any such thing. All he does is take orders. When he plays, he plays to enjoy at least one realm in which he does not have to comply with the wishes of another.

Still another theory says that play is the activity in

and by which we fulfill wishes. We play and vicariously become the pilot, hunter, doctor, business tycoon, race car driver, etc. I might play because of an innate desire to compete. Perhaps that need for competition is not met by my job.

All these theories are interesting and any one could be the foundation of a separate study. No theory, however, explains fully why we play. There seems to be an undeniable spirit of play in us. If we experience healthy competition on our jobs, we still play a fierce game of tennis on the weekend. Why is that? We do not need an answer to this question today. We are able to function without an answer. In fact, thinking you must justify your play will make you reluctant to encourage it. Some of what play does for us is as difficult to see as the reason we play.

In seminary I took a course on the often obtuse theology of Paul Tillich. I confessed to my professor the belief that this "stuff" would be hard to preach. His answer was unforgettable and provocative. He said we did not study Tillich to preach Tillich, but to have Tillich inform our other preaching and teaching. In the same way, we do not play to see the immediate, direct value of play, but to allow the divergent rhythm of play to inform our other areas of life.

Play seems to be an extravagant waste of a precious commodity.

From an accounting viewpoint we cannot often justify play. We must spend our time wisely and that means getting through the agenda, making resolutions, handing out assignments, hearing reports, etc. Once we understand that the investment in play is an investment in the more obvious parts of our agenda, we are freed to play with abandon.

When I was in the pastorate, I had a staff member who was a fellow logophile. We enjoyed playing Scrabble and showing off our newly-acquired words. We usually played during office hours and, I must confess, I felt guilty playing a game during the time I was being paid to write sermons, Bible studies, counsel, or get ready for the next all-night board meeting.

On one occasion my secretary asked what she should say if someone called while my associate and I played Scrabble. I told her she could either tell them I was in a board meeting (which is true of any gathering around a Scrabble board) or that I was working on some letters (which are the basic equipment of any such game). Actually, she simply told them I was in a meeting. Those games gave me and that staff member a level on which to relate that we would not have had otherwise. Rather than wasting time, the game became a team-building exercise. I did not want to be disturbed, because that time was just as beneficial as a "straight" meeting would be.

When we rush through our recreational times as if they were preliminaries, we make a great error. Often the playtime is the very door through which fresh insight comes. Despise not the light-hearted times!

Have you ever considered your vacation a part of your work? That the leisure contributes to your industriousness?

Having been a fan of comedy since I was a child, I

enjoy reading through joke books, listening to stand-up comics, and reading anecdotes with a punchline. I seek out these stories if they do not find their way to me. I ask people what jokes they've heard lately. This is not being frivolous. It is an attempt to feed the part of me that is ever at play. That stream of comedy, of play, of lightness, is a feeder stream for my more profound thoughts.

We would do well to see play as an investment rather than a waste. In his wonderful book on creativity, *A Whack on the Side of the Head*, Roger von Oech speaks of the value of play. After asking thousands of people to identify the situations in which they get most of their ideas, von Oech observed that two settings are most common. Some get their ideas as a result of thinking about a specific problem. Others generate fresh ideas as they are fooling around or toying with a problem. This led von Oech to conclude:

> Necessity may be the mother of invention, but play is certainly the father. . . . Most of life presents you with a win/lose proposition: if you don't win, you lose. This is true for most games and sporting events, elections, coin-tosses, bets, arguments, and the like. When you play, however, a different logic is at work: a win/no win logic. This is an important difference because it means that instead of being penalized for our mistakes, we learn from them. Thus when we win, we win, when we don't, we learn. This is a nice arrangement; the only thing play costs is the time to do it.[1]

CHAPTER 4

Frequently in our thinking, we stop just short of an exciting burst of innovation. To understand the spirit of play is to push the limits and refrain from stopping your thinking just because it has gotten weird or silly. Often, it is at that precise moment that the "good stuff" comes. I encourage participants in my creativity workshops to play with an idea until it seems absurd and then (and only then) they should sprinkle in some realism. Play forces us beyond our safety zones and out into the risky waters of "unusual thinking." It is precisely in the arena of absurdity that many of our best ideas are born.

You own a house with a large yard. Every autumn, with great frustration, you set your hand to the task of leaf removal. Play with an alternate way to remove the leaves, besides raking them. Be crazy in your ideas. Imagine there are no budgetary, mechanical, or personnel limitations. Go ahead, design a way to remove those leaves. At the end of the chapter, I'll give you some suggestions that have come from workshops I've conducted where this problem has been given.[2]

CHAPTER 4

Having argued for play that is non-utilitarian, let me also argue that some forms of play are more creativity-enhancing than others. There are games and leisure activities that require no thinking at all.

Those games do not demand our interaction or strategizing. While they would not, on that basis alone, be deemed worthless, there are other games which contribute to our ability to see differently. For example, crossword puzzles force us to survey our vocabulary, play with word forms, and eliminate options as we sweep our storehouse of words.

Charades is another game that pulls at our ability to generate ideas. Painting and drawing in one's leisure is

another way to enhance creativity while playing. If these things be true, choose play that engages you.

Far from being a break in the day of our normal routine, play is a method of getting at some truths or some data. Play is not the art of doing nothing; it is the art of doing something seemingly unconnected to the life task. In a classic contribution to the field, Johan Huizinga suggests there are three main characteristics of play:

1. Play is a voluntary, free activity.
2. Play is distinct from "ordinary" or "real" life.
3. Play is limited in locality and duration.[3]

Since play is in a realm by itself, we need not try to align it with the rest of life. We enjoy it for the break it gives us; for the insight we gain from it. Huizinga says play has its own location, either material or ideal. We leave the playground (actual or mental) and return to "real" life. If this is true, then our efforts to justify the trip to playland are futile. Simply enjoy!

From where I sit, it appears that the line between work and play keeps shifting, if not disappearing. Some of us so enjoy our work that it seems like play. Others so abhor play that they must work at it. Shall we work or shall we play? God has created us for both. Know the difference (where there is one) and do both to the glory of the God who worked at creation and then pronounced it good!

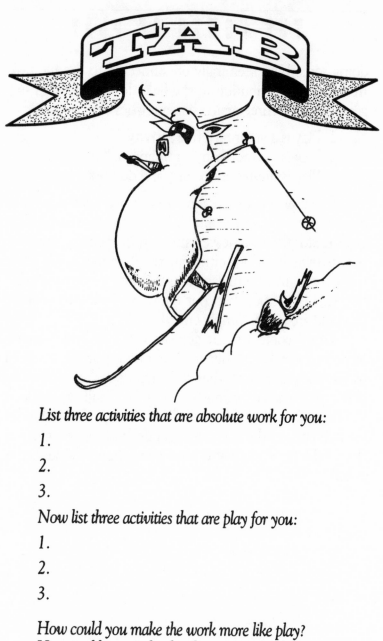

List three activities that are absolute work for you:

1.

2.

3.

Now list three activities that are play for you:

1.

2.

3.

How could you make the work more like play?
How could you make the play more serious?

Notes

1. Roger von Oech, *A Whack on the Side of the Head* (New York: Warner Books, 1982).

2. Suggestions for leaf removal:

• *Invite an elementary school class to your yard for a leaf-collecting field trip.*

• *Have a neighborhood party to which each person must bring a trash bag. Each participant takes a bag of leaves home.*

• *Have a barbecue, using the burning leaves as the fire fuel.*

• *Invite a youth group over to your home, spray each member with adhesive, have them roll in the leaves and send them home.*

• *Hide items of value in the leaves and sponsor a scavenger hunt for neighbors. Everyone who finds a prize takes the prize and a bag of leaves home.*

• *Bag the leaves and sell them as mulch.*

• *Contact a detention facility and offer a work experience for some residents—what a great citizen you are to allow the residents to rake your yard!*

3. Johan Huizinga, *Homo Ludens* (Boston: Beacon Press, 1950), 8-9.

RULES: MADE TO BE BROKEN, BENT, AND CHALLENGED

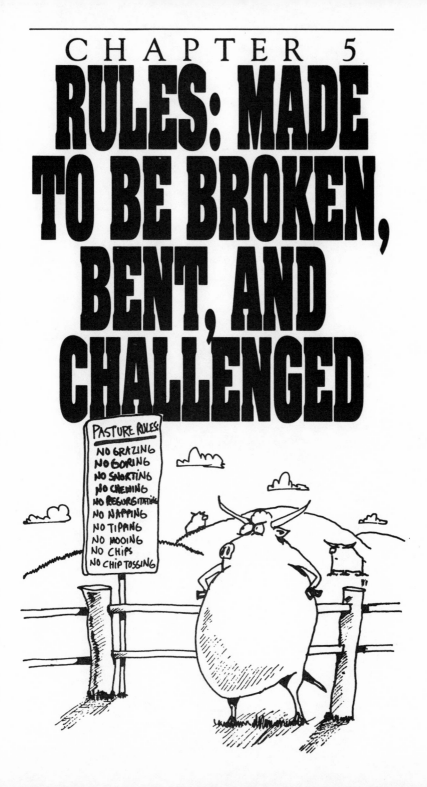

PASTURE RULES:

NO GRAZING
NO GORING
NO SNORTING
NO CHEWING
NO REGURGITATING
NO NAPPING
NO TIPPING
NO MOOING
NO CHIPS
NO CHIP TOSSING

RULES: MADE TO BE BROKEN

ou can't grow up in any culture and not be exposed to rules. Some that I remember are:

- Don't talk with your mouth full.
- Don't enter your sister's room without knocking.
- Don't chew with your mouth open.
- No singing at the table.
- No TV until your homework is done.
- If you empty the water jar in the refrigerator you must refill it (this rule accounted for the teaspoon of water left in the jar).
- Don't talk to strangers.
- Don't go to anybody's house without permission.
- Don't talk back to your mother (unless you have a strong desire to lose teeth).
- Make your bed before you go out.
- Always wear clean underwear because you might be in a car accident. (Frankly, this rule made the least sense to me. I still can't imagine an ambulance driver taking note of the cleanliness of my BVDs.)
- No dessert before you finish your vegetables.

The Bible has its share of rules as well:
- Let all things be done properly and in an orderly manner (1 Corinthians 14:40).
- Do not grieve the Holy Spirit of God (Ephesians 4:30).
- Be kind to one another (Ephesians 4:32).

- Forgive one another (Ephesians 4:32).
- Speak truth, each one of you with his neighbor (Ephesians 4:25).
- Always rejoice (1 Thessalonians 5:16).
- Always pray (1 Thessalonians 5:17).
- Always give thanks (1 Thessalonians 5:18).
- Go into all the world and preach [proclaim] the gospel to all creation (Mark 16:15).
- If anyone wishes to come after me [Jesus], let him deny himself, and take up his cross, and follow me (Mark 8:34).
- Love one another, just as I have loved you (John 15:12).
- Render to all what is due them; tax to whom tax is due; custom to whom custom; fear to whom fear; honor to whom honor (Romans 13:7).
- Do not love the world, nor the things in the world (1 John 2:15).

Given a blank piece of paper and thirty to forty minutes, you could think of at least one hundred rules from *your* background. Recalling the rules from the Bible might take a little longer and require a concordance, but you get the point. Our natural responses to rules are three:

1. Keep (obey) the rule.
2. Challenge (bend) the rule.
3. Break (disobey) the rule.

Points two and three are not synonymous. Some rules are not easily understood or they do not make sense to the doer. If a reasonable explanation is given, it is often enough to command obedience. The rule-reader is not saying, "I will not obey this rule." He or she is saying, "I don't understand this rule. Explain it to me so I can decide if I'll obey it or not." With the dozen rules from my childhood I did that quite a bit. I didn't usually get answers that satisfied me but I was not articulate, brave, or foolish enough to challenge them. Now that I'm older let me ask, "Why *can't* we eat our dessert first?"

I have heard of progressive suppers in which we eat each course at a different home. It is a great way for a group to spend an evening together. Have you ever heard of a *regressive* supper? It starts with dessert at one member's home and regresses to the final home where you enjoy appetizers. You would have to challenge a rule (which does not have to be kept) in order to have such a dinner.

With the biblical rules we have the same options but must operate with caution. Disobedience (option 3) is not part of the serious disciple's tool kit. However, as we keep the rules of God, we have more latitude than we may have realized. "Love one another" is a rule, but precisely *how* we do that is left to our creativity. True, it is to be as Christ loved us. However, that being so expansive, there is great room for our ingenuity. How about planning a hug attack for one of your friends? You and ten others sneak up on the person and smother him or her with physical and verbal love. Too radical? Relax. It was just a suggestion.

What are the rules in your church, parachurch organization, corporation, school, home? Should they be faithfully, unswervingly obeyed? Cautiously challenged? Defiantly broken? Behold some "rules" of a church in Anywhere, U.S.A.:

- Morning worship begins at 11:00 A.M.
- We must have announcements in that worship service.
- Only the adult choir sings at the "main service."
- We'll only sing hymns we know and love.
- If we begin at 11:00 A.M., we must conclude no later than 12:15 P.M.
- Only women are active in the missionary support/missionary circle.
- The sermon must have three alliterative points.
- We must have an altar call (invitation) at every service.
- Men must wear ties. Women must wear dresses.

- Communion/The Lord's Supper must be served on the first Sunday of each month.
- The pastor's wife must lead the Women's Bible class.
- The pastor's wife must play the piano.

A pastor started a church outside Pittsburgh, Pennsylvania, recently. Sunday worship begins at 2:00 P.M. Imagine that! They broke the rule. When asked to defend this violation, the pastor said his folks liked to sleep a little late on Sunday mornings, eat a leisurely breakfast, and then prepare for worship. Apparently scores of others think his idea is good. Now, brace yourself—do you think you could bend, challenge, or even break some rules in *your* church?

Minister of Music

Does the prelude have to be played on a keyboard instrument, by an adult? Does the choir have to sing from the left? From the front? Must we save all our Advent music for December? Would the congregation sing if no one stood in front of them waving his/her hands?

Parachurch Organization Leader

Does every person in your organization have to "raise" his/her support? Are there never exceptions to that policy? Do all chapters, units, clubs, clusters, or regions of your organization have to look the same? Should there be a separate department for specialized groups? Must there be?

CHAPTER 5

Preacher

Must you always use the same translation in study or in preaching? Must every sermon be formatted the same way? Do you always have to preach from the pulpit? Must you always be standing?

Missions Leader

Does the Missions Conference have to begin on the same day of the week each year? Must the missionaries always bring slides? Must we sing the same mission hymns and choruses each year?

Christian Educator

Does Sunday school have to be held on Sunday? Does the lesson have to be taught "on schedule"? Do primary and junior students always have to be separated from each other? Do senior citizens always have to be taught by the lecture/discussion method? Could they have arts and crafts time, too?

Ushers

Do visitors have to wear a name tag to receive attention or a visitor's packet? Does the main floor have to be filled before we open the balcony? Must we seat people in such a way that the sanctuary is filled symmetrically? Does the offering have to be taken by men? By adults?

In virtually every area of congregational/organizational life, there are rules to be read, questions to be asked, and decisions to be made. I am not going to give answers to the questions raised, but I do want to prompt you to take some on. Let me offer just one "suppose" in each of the previously mentioned categories. You must do the rest. With a group of open-minded, non-threatened people (don't ask me where you would find such a group), you could have one of the most significant meetings of the year as you look at the rules and then challenge them, bend them and yes, even break them.

Minister of Music

Suppose you survey all the children who take instrumental music lessons in school. Choose four of them to do the preludes for the next month, one per Sunday. Afraid they won't play perfectly? Perfection is rare . . . even in adults.

Domestic Engineer/Homemaker

Suppose all tasks in the home were tied to a life principle that was clearly articulated by you when that task is being done or is completed. What would happen if the child learned not only to take out the garbage but we talked with the child about the garbage? Such a conversation could lead to significant dialogue about the environment, responsibility, vermin, and waste.

Preacher

Suppose you preached a two-point sermon on a stool from the main floor of the worship space, rather than high and lifted up. Afraid the people won't respect the casual approach? You might be pleasantly surprised by their positive reception to an occasional change of physical setting.

Mission Leader

Suppose we had a mission *season* rather than a conference, with emphases spread over the autumn and closing on Thanksgiving Day. You might see an increase in faith promise giving or mission pledges as people connect world evangelization with Thanksgiving.

Christian Educator

Suppose you held all classes on Wednesday or Saturday evenings, to alleviate the rushed feeling of Sunday morning classes. Even a trial run of this idea might yield surprising results.

Parachurch Leader

Suppose you created a category or strategy for those who are not as adept at fund-raising as others. A mission organization I serve recently sent a financially under-supported family to South America as short-termers with few amenities, even though they wanted to go as career missionaries. This was an alternative to having that family rust here while continually stumping around the country raising support.

Usher

Suppose you offered every worshiper a visitor's packet at the door so that visitors didn't stick out in the morning worship unless they wanted to. Those who are members will refuse the packets and visitors will take it, if interested.

Much of our ability to be generative is stifled because of our submission to the rules. A creative person is not one who is extraordinarily gifted (whatever *that* is), but rather, one who is training his/her eyes to see. What's changing around me? How may I respond to those changes? Is my current way of doing things keeping me challenged, fresh, on the "cutting edge" of my profession, ministry? What risks are involved if I break the rules? Who will be affected, offended, liberated?

Some rules are outdated, culturally irrelevant, and harmful by now. I cannot tell you what they are for you. I could suggest some and you might agree with me. However, so many of the rules which inform your creativity or failure to express your creativity are peculiar to your environment. Of such rules I may be ignorant. Wondrous experiences come out of some rule-challenging. Putting your opinion regarding twentieth-century music aside, is it not fascinating to hear how Stravinsky, Prokofiev, Gershwin, and Cage have approached rules of music? They kept pushing and pushing until they exceeded the boundaries of "proper" music.

Whether or not you'd call Picasso a great artist, you must admire his "different way of seeing."

I am writing some of these chapters while traveling. As I write today, I am in one of the hotels of a major chain. As most hotels do,

CHAPTER 5

they suffer the loss of many towels each year. In the bath today, I found a bright, well-designed drawing of three towels with faces—a family hanging on a towel bar. Beneath the drawing was written:

> The other day, the towels told us they were being kidnaped and taken to faraway places. So we adopted new ones and everyone's happy again. Now you wouldn't want to break up a new family?

What a creative way to address the old problem of towel-klepto. Isn't that several cuts above a sign that reads, in block letters, "PLEASE DO NOT REMOVE TOWELS FROM THE ROOM"? Some creative person broke hotel management's rule regarding how to appeal to guests.

Now, before you go commit anarchy, let's take time for another T.A.B.

List five rules of your church, company, organization. Then rank each rule as follows:

1 = should not be challenged or broken.

2 = could and should be changed, with some difficulty; probably will not happen in my lifetime; might happen when the moon turns striped purple and all cows fly.

3 = could and should be changed easily; a pushover.

Don't go any further until you've done this exercise, alone or in a small group.

CHAPTER 5

Are you continuing to read on without doing the T.A.B.? Pause. The writing down of the rules will help you analyze your situation. Do it now! What did you discover? Certainly you had no trouble thinking of five items. The most difficult part of the exercise was judgment. Doctrinal belief and history may occasion the assignment of a 1. The twos and threes are more difficult. See, with the assignment of a 1 to any rule, the only proper response is continued obedience . . . keeping the rule. Assigning a 2 or 3 to any item, however, places a responsibility upon us. We must *do* something. The reason it is so crucial to write your list is because you cannot break, bend, challenge, or obey until you know the rule! Creative writers must know what a sonnet is, how to write a standard paragraph, a first person article, and a limerick, before they can confidently strike out on their own. It is knowing the rules that allows us the courage and confidence to break, bend, challenge, and obey.

This may account for why church renewal is accomplished more frequently by the lovers of the church than by its critics. Those of us on the inside have learned the rules. We obey some but break others, *with care.*

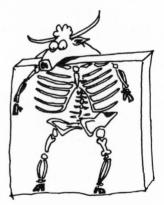

Creativity is not being careless, insensitive, or rude. It is not always doing wild, crazy,

off-the-wall things (although it may take that form). It's
seeing differently. Youth workers often burn the midnight
oil dreaming up the next kooky event to keep their kids
interested. That's not necessarily creativity. So open your
eyes, look around. Look inside. Look outside. Look at the
underside. Take aerial shots, X-rays. The more views you
get, the more creative you'll be. Is your hand raised high
yet?

The most radical response to rules is to challenge,
break, or bend them, so it seems. The saddest response is
to keep and obey them, without ever knowing why.

I can still hear our Lord saying to a confused woman,
"You worship that which you do not know" (John 4:22a,
NASB). Might the same be said of our rules?

CHAPTER 6
I THOUGHT IT, BUT I'D NEVER SAY IT

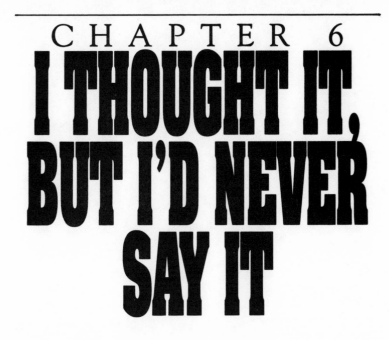

e all have, in the backs of our minds, some possible solutions to problems that we dare not bring up. There are any number of reasons:

1. The solution might be personally embarrassing.
2. The solution might embarrass a colleague.
3. The solution might be labeled "silly" or "impractical."
4. The solution might violate some written or "understood" social or cultural rule.

It is this idea of coming against that which is *taboo* that prompts James Adams, in his book *Conceptual Blockbusting*, to make use of a great creativity exercise. I have tried it with groups in my creativity workshops and it always produces results that give new meaning to the word "interesting."

Assume that a steel pipe is embedded in the concrete floor of a bare room as shown below:

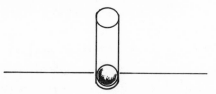

The inside diameter is .06" larger than the diameter of a Ping-Pong ball (1.5") that rests gently at the bottom of the pipe. You are one of a group of six people in the room, along with the following objects:

CHAPTER 6

100' of clothesline
A carpenter's hammer
A chisel
A box of Wheaties
A file
A wire coat hanger
A monkey wrench
A light bulb

List as many ways as you can think of (in five minutes) to get the ball out of the pipe without damaging the ball, tube, or floor.[1]

Before you read further, why not try this one yourself? No, seriously, put the book down and give it a shot. Generate as many ideas as come to your mind, whether they "make sense" or not. Allow me to reproduce the following lengthy quote in which Adams explains his use of the exercise:

> J. P. Guilford, one of the pioneers in the study of creativity, speaks a great deal about fluency and flexibility of thought. *Fluency* refers to the number of concepts one produces in a given length of time. If you are a fluent thinker, you have a long list of methods of retrieving the ball from the pipe. However, quantity is only part of the game. *Flexibility* refers to the diversity of the ideas generated. If you are a flexible thinker, you should have come up with a wide variety of methods. If you thought of filing the wire coat hanger in two, flattening the resulting ends, and making large tweezers to retrieve the ball, you

came up with a solution to the problem, but a fairly common one. If you thought of smashing the handle of the hammer with the monkey wrench and using the resulting splinters to retrieve the ball, you were demonstrating a bit more flexibility of thought, since one does not usually think of using a tool as a source of splinters to do something with. If you managed to do something with the Wheaties you are an even more flexible thinker.

Did you think of having your group urinate in the pipe? If you did not think of this, why not? The answer is probably a cultural block, in this case a *taboo*, since urinating is somewhat of a closet activity in the U.S.

. . . I have used this Ping-Pong ball exercise with many groups and the response is not only a function of our culture, but also of the particular people in the group and the particular ambiance of the meeting. A mixed group newly convened in elegant surroundings will seldom think of urinating in the pipe. Even if members in the group do come up with this as a solution, they will keep very quiet about it. A group of people who work together, especially if all-male and it's at the end of the working session, will instantly break into delighted chortles as they think of this and equally gross solutions. The importance of this answer is not that urinating in the pipe is necessarily the best of all solutions to the problem (although it is certainly a good one), but rather that cultural taboos can remove entire families of solutions from the ready grasp of the problem-solver. Taboos therefore are conceptual blocks.[2]

Not too long ago, one never saw commercials on television for feminine hygiene products. Although we all knew they were purchased, we didn't talk about them or see advertisements for them. Today such ads are common. What happened? Someone confronted a taboo.

As we discussed earlier, every organization or congregation has its own rules, its own culture. As that entity takes on a life of its own, it also develops no-no's, subjects not to be brought up. Not merely a matter of challenging the status quo, as with a rule, a taboo is that which may not even be brought up for discussion. One of the differences between a taboo and a rule is that the consequences for breaking a taboo may be less severe than for those for breaking a rule. The breaking of a taboo incurs no legal or administrative penalties. However, the societal offense may be just as strong. Another difference is that rules are articulated so that all members of the group, class, culture, or sub-culture know what is expected of them. What are the taboos in your company? In your home? In your church?

Taboos are the things you think about but might not utter. I was thinking about my growing up and some of the unspoken expectations with which I was surrounded:

1. In our church, we don't call the pastor by his first name . . . ever!

2. We don't touch other people in certain parts
   of their anatomy.
3. We don't pick our noses in public.
4. We don't eat food out of the garbage.
5. We don't go outside without underwear on.

I don't recall anyone ever sitting me down and going over these. I've simply known, for what seems like all my life, that these were unacceptable activities. After a period of time, the taboos succeed in shutting down an entire set of options for us. We might think it but we'd never say it.

In my Baptist upbringing, although it was never stated, a deacon was an ordained layman who enjoyed great respect and prestige in the local congregation. Short of a highly public sin, deacons were not removed from the deacon board. In fact, in some congregations a deacon's ineffectiveness would be overlooked to avoid the high political price confrontation would exact. If a group of people from such a congregation were to brainstorm about how they could improve the congregational perception of the deacon board, firing a deacon might never be brought up. In the group's opinion, that man is in place for life. Therefore, what could happen if the board were relieved of the men who are no longer effective is not seriously considered.

An embarrassing list for us to write might be one containing all the opportunities we have missed because of the taboos in our cultural or sub-cultural group. What shall we do to break free of the taboos that bind us?

Warning: Confronting taboos may be hazardous to your sense of security!

In fact, you feel like a traitor the moment you start confronting the "forbidden fruit" of your culture. For two years immediately after graduation from college, I served on the administrative staff of that college. One of my privileges was to call my colleagues by their first names. It was a strange shift and I felt disrespectful as I found myself calling by first name, a professor whom I'd addressed as Dr. Jones just a month or two earlier.

As you look at the no-no's of your situation, imagine a worst case scenario. What would happen if you *did* do the forbidden thing? What are the consequences of saying those things which (it is understood) "we never say"? Having looked at the very worst that could happen, are you ready to risk it? Let me give you my 3-D program for opening the treasure chest of options that taboos have kept closed before us.

1. Determine what the taboos are in your culture or sub-cultural group. There may be only one. There may be dozens. You don't know what they are? Ask around. Dig, scoop, inquire.

2. Decide that they are *at least* worth examining and challenging. Because so much lies hidden behind and beyond the taboos, simply decide that you cannot afford *not* to consider violating them.

3. Defer action if you can't/won't pay the price of that action. Part of creative thinking is being willing to take the risks that come with the territory. You must always have some level of comfort after you've made the most difficult decisions. You do need some sense of creative tension to keep the juices of creativity flowing, but you do not need anxiety at every turn. If the challenge of the norm and taboos makes you afraid to proceed, don't!

A few years ago I went to the meeting of the Christian education board of the church I pastored. It was in the fall and we were beginning to talk about our annual Christmas program. Each year, previously, we would sponsor an evening consisting of a brief presentation by each class, followed by a meal. It was one of those evenings few enjoyed except, perhaps, the parents of those cute children who recited:

> Jesus was born on Christmas day
> Our hearts he did make glad.
> If he had not been born this day
> We would be very sad.

CHAPTER 6

I asked the board if it would like to try something different that year. You need to know that by that time, the board knew that such a question, coming from me, was dangerous. The danger notwithstanding, board members said yes. We started by talking about the purpose of the Christmas program. It was designed to:

1. Affirm, for and with Christians, the joy of the birth of Christ.

2. To reach those families that did not regularly attend our church but who *would* come out to see their children perform.

3. To make a statement to our neighbors about what we believed regarding the birth of Christ.

We fundamentally agreed that purpose three was not being fulfilled at all. Outsiders did not attend our program unless they had a vested interest (a performing child) in the program. We decided to look at an alternative program for the Christmas season. That was risky simply because of one of the unspoken rules around that church: *Don't tamper with the Christmas program.*

We eventually decided upon an outdoor manger scene that would be set up for several nights, which would entice outsiders to come see what for us was "the reason for the season." Outdoor manger scenes are commonplace in some towns, but it was not common for our neighborhood. Our church building was landlocked and we had not one blade of grass to call our own. We had no lawn, no sprawling acreage, and no hill from which to proclaim these grand ideas. We did, however, have an idea.

Opposite our building we had a graveled parking lot. Borrowing two sheep from a farm outside Pittsburgh, we tethered the sheep in the lot, placed some hay on the ground, dressed ourselves in Palestinian-looking garments, played Christmas carols over a public address system, handed out literature about the meaning of the birth of Christ, and demonstrated our joy for several nights. Simultaneously, we had volunteers across the street in the church building hosting a "cafe." If one of us on the street engaged a passerby in significant dialogue, we could invite him or her indoors for a cup of hot chocolate, a few cookies, and continued conversation. It was most memorable!

An interesting note was that we were afraid to leave the sheep outdoors for those days . . . not because the sheep couldn't handle the cold, but because we feared for their safety. So we put them in the men's room of the

church each night after our presentation. Our men remembered those sheep for weeks after they were gone.

One of our teachers insisted that while this might have been a creative approach to Christmas, there was still a need for "the regular Christmas program." She did have such an evening and all was well. Although most people who attended our manger scene enjoyed it, it was risky on our parts because it challenged a sacred cow. How dare we tamper with a proven tradition? No one ever told me that we should not disturb the traditional structure, but that was made evident by the repetition of the annual event.

Is there an exciting variation on a traditional event that is deep inside you but you've squashed it until now? Take a piece of paper and play with the idea. That's a beginning. What are the *genuine* risks? Exactly *how many* traditions will this disturb?

A Final Word

Often what prevents us from tackling the taboos is not fear, but laziness. If something works it is easier for us to simply fill in the blanks and serve it up again. Being fresh demands more of us. Have you come to the planning of an activity and essentially done the same thing as was done last year, with the exception of changing the players, the readers, the musical selections? Was this year's award banquet a replica of last year's? It may not be because you didn't want to challenge the rules or the taboos, but simply because you didn't want to knock yourself out with the extra work required. Being innovative and creative takes much work! Make the commitment, now, to spend yourself in pursuit of that which is nonstale and non-predictable.

Notes

1. James Adams, *Conceptual Blockbusting* (New York: W.W. Norton, 1974), 54.
2. Ibid., 54-55.

CHAPTER 7
A CUE FROM THE OBVIOUS

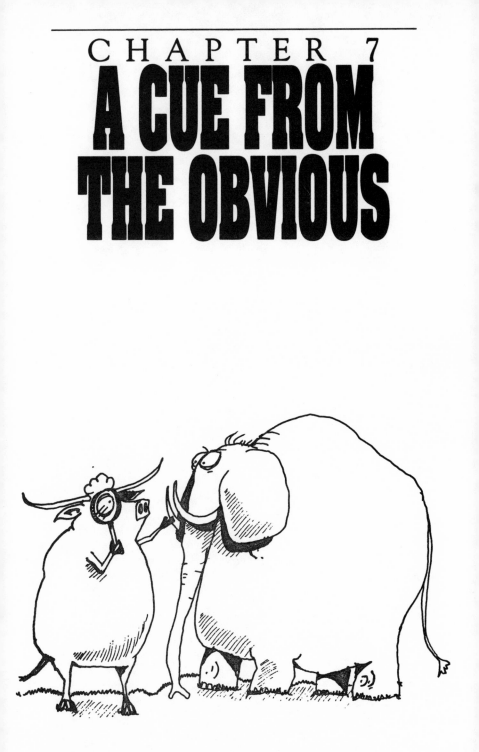

iscard those ideas of brilliant, absent-minded professors squirrelled away in laboratories, emerging after months, proudly displaying their latest inventions. Most of us need a context full of humans in which to create. We don't generally create in a vacuum. I thought to ignore the role of others in the creative process but I cannot. Those around us enhance or stifle our innovation. Their effect on us may be direct or subtle. But there is no such thing as creating while being unaffected by those who make up our surroundings.

You may have a secretary who guards your time and privacy so you can write or read. There is the spouse who sees that your basement workshop is not entered without permission. The "go-fer" who keeps your pencils sharpened, your coffee cup filled, your desk clean, your needed research tools nearby, your paints at the ready, fresh paper in your typewriter, flour and sugar in your pantry, or clay in your studio is directly affecting your creative output. So is the skeptic who dismisses every one of your new ideas, the family member who reminds you that you tried that once before and failed, the bank manager who turns down your loan application, and the "friends" who withhold praise until after you've succeeded.

You are always pushed *along* by some and pushed *aside* by others. Every person in your world contributes something (even if that something is negative) to your life's symphony.

It is then critical that we learn to read those around us. Whether they be friend or foe, they can be valuable to

CHAPTER 7

us. If they be marked by words that motivate, encourage, affirm, and stimulate, they become our sounding boards, our let-me-bounce-some-ideas-off-you people. But there's even great use for the dismal, negative, the glass-is-half-empty folks in your world. They bring out the healthy pride in us. They spur us on when we would quit. If I'm slightly lethargic, the thought that someone out there is counting on my failure gets me moving!

Put motivation aside for a moment. It would be ideal if I were so committed to my craft that I'd do my best regardless of who's watching me. Let's say that isn't the case right now. Just knowing that old Harvey Beeswax said, "Richard will never be able to pull it off" gets my engine revved.

I've never taken bowling too seriously. I bowl for fun and don't invest too much energy in the mastery of it. But I've discovered that I'm a much better bowler on a Friday night in a packed bowling alley when people are watching than I am in a sparsely populated one on a weekday afternoon. The people around me affect my score . . . somewhat. They draw the last ounce of concentration out of me. I try not to give them cause for snickering.

Therefore, since the people around us so affect our productivity, the more we know about them the better off we are.

Write down the names of six people who most directly affect your output. Whose desks are near yours at work? Who are the members of the service clubs to which you belong? Who is your art teacher? Who is the first person to hear or see your new ideas? Who reports to you regularly? To whom do you report? Who attends your brainstorming sessions?

On a sheet of paper draw three vertical columns. In column one, put the person's name. In column two, put a P or N for positive or negative influence on you. In the final column draw any graphic representation of that person that comes to mind.

My friend Mephibosheth is always encouraging me. His line looks like this:

Mephibosheth | P |

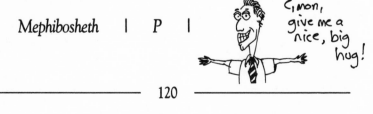

A CUE FROM THE OBVIOUS

Now every time I see Mephibosheth in my mind's eye, I see him as a bright spot in my day. I will be more inclined to run flashes of thought and insight by him than by someone whose line looks like this:

Leo | N |

Don't proceed until you do this, because the sooner you know your immediate creativity context, the more immediate will be your strategic use of it.

❖

Sometimes without saying a word, those around us give us permission to create or suggest that innovation is not a good idea. In a sense, throughout our lives we are writing a symphony. Each measure is hammered out, edited and rearranged as we live out our days. The people around us affect the notes, the rhythm, the harmony. Let me introduce you to eight types of persons in our world who either keep the music going or try to stuff a sock in the bells of our french horns.

Horace Whole Note | P |

This is the man who will endure when others quit. He's steady, dependable, solid, loyal. Many have been taught that a whole note gets four beats. That's not always true. What *is* important is that we understand it in relation to other notes.

A whole note gets held twice as long as a half note (♩), four times as long as a quarter note (♩), eight times as long as an eighth note (♪), and sixteen times as long as sixteenth notes (♪). That is, when others drop out, Horace hangs in there.

Every inventor needs a Horace. He is the able assistant who stays with you through the failed experiments. It is not that Horace is brilliant, but that he's tenacious. He's willing to hang on with you.

You must understand how to use Horace. You don't run to him for immediate, enthusiastic hoopla. He's the guy who is there for you when the party is over. He's the faithful one who helps you clean up.

Is he valuable? Oh yes!! Does he affect your output? Undoubtedly! If your creativity context is full of Horaces, there will be a certain texture of confidence to your projects. You will not feel as if you're alone. The short bursts of discouragement will be balanced by the steady support of your whole note peer.

Fanny Fermata | N |

Do you remember that funny-looking musical symbol? It gives the conductor license to hold a note eternally. Any note with a fermata over its head is in no rush to let go. That note is out of step with the others. Other measures move on in predictable time, but a measure with a fermata takes its time.

In your creativity context, there are people who can't or won't move along. Cautious to a fault, they analyze, reevaluate, do a study on, have a meeting about, and generally sap the energy from most ideas. They put everything on hold. Under the guise of helping you not to move "too fast" they don't move at all.

There are any number of reasons why the Fanny

Fermatas of our world are the way they are. They may have a strong fear of failure . . . or success (see chapter 11). Perhaps they suggest that you will succeed and they will, in comparison, look deficient. For whatever reason, they try to convince you that "this does not seem to reflect sound judgment at this particular point in time," or that "the risk factor is too high in this instance and extreme caution should be exercised."

Rachel Rest | P |

Do you tend toward workaholism? Rachel is the person in your life who reminds you to live the balanced life. She's the faithful friend who says "even if you stay at the office twenty hours a day for thirty-two years, there will be work to do—so why not take a few days off?" She would give you, for your birthday, the plaque that reads:

> Sometimes when you're feeling important
> Sometimes when your ego's in bloom
> Sometimes when you take it for granted
> you're the most qualified in the room
> Sometimes when you feel your going
> would leave an unfillable hole
> just follow this simple instruction
> and see how it humbles your soul
> Take a bucket and fill it with water
> put your hand in it up to your wrist
> Take it out and the hole that's remaining
> is a measure of how you'll be missed

You can splash all you please as you enter
You can stir up the water galore
But stop and you'll find in a minute
that it looks quite the same as before
There's a moral in this quaint example
Just do the best that you can
Be proud of yourself but remember
There is no indispensable man

As life's symphony is played out, the function of Rachel is to remind us that it is acceptable to have a few measures of silence, of reflection. She says the music can stop for a moment and the integrity of the piece won't be damaged. She's the dramatic, refreshing pause at the end of the Hallelujah chorus. Have you sung it? You know the very end where the novices at the sing-along sing one more "hallelujah"? The rest is so-o-o-o-o-o effective there. We have been belting out the proclamation: "And he shall reign for ever and ever, hallelujah." Just before we say it one last time, let's take a breath.

MAZON is a program that invites American Jews to add 3 percent to the costs of joyous celebrations (a bar or bat mitzvah, wedding, birthday, anniversary) and donate that money to the alleviation of hunger. Rather than simply making celebrative families feel guilty because they are "haves" in an world of "have nots," MAZON offers a creative response. Leonard Fein, the founder of MAZON, not only saw occasions where quantities of food were consumed but also the great problem of hunger in our land. As he saw both problems differently, he came up with a way to have one affect the other.

That breath is Rachel. She's the person in your world who forces you to pause just when you go at your task again. She's the colleague who arranges a morning where you have no appointments if the previous day was a hectic one. She's the spouse who buys two tickets to a weekend festival whether you thought you could squeeze it in or not. She's the five-year-old who won't let you believe your own press releases and invites you to her room to sit in miniature chairs to "have tea." Rachel provides perspective for women and men who envision the world caving in if they dare miss a beat.

Steven Staccato | N |

The primary quality of a staccato passage in a symphony is that, compared to a long, fluid passage, it is short, sharp, detached. The notes don't run into each other. Each note in such a passage stands alone. In your creative world there are some who will rarely, if ever, work with you. They will not usually seek to cooperate with you. They stand alone like a monument to self-help. Their hero is the Lone Ranger.

Steven shows himself in an inability or unwillingness to be a part of the team. He holds up the otherwise unanimous enthusiasm for a project. He's the dissenting vote on most board decisions. When everyone else is full of vision, he "can't see it." When Steven speaks, the language is radically different from that of his peers. He's short-sighted, possessed by a sharp tongue and not connected to what's going on. He's the guy who listens to a thirty-minute presentation and then asks a question that has nothing to do with what the rest of us just heard.

Steven serves as a constant, visible reminder that not everyone is sold on my idea; that the whole world isn't waiting for my next pronouncement, composition, or product. Steven stands apart from the mainstream, on the outside looking in. His detachment need not be a deterrent.

Terrance Tutti | P |

Occasionally in life's musical score you'll see the word *tutti*. Italian for "together," it's the signal for all instruments that have either been soloing or resting, to play together now. Terrance is the man in your world who brings the disparate elements together. He's the resource person who pulls in a little of this and a little of that. He crosses departmental, divisional, regional, denominational, ethnic, linguistic, and experiential lines to get the job done.

He's the one who suggests a sub-contractor outside the favored circle. He hires a consultant for a project just to get a new angle. He isn't hesitant to bring in a child to speak with an adult group, in order to gain fresh insight. He designs and distributes a survey to solicit ideas from other levels of workers in the company.

Terrance is always interested in what things would look like if we had more variety. He doesn't get excited about one violin. He longs to hear the lush sound of a string section. He wants to hear the sound of the tubas playing with the cellos. His ears perk up when he hears a blend, a combination of sounds. He draws on the best of all known and available worlds of ideas. Terrance is the dabbler. He entertains a splash of color here, a novel approach there, a fresh voice here. His aim? To hear all the instruments play in concert.

Reuben Rubato

Now just hold on everyone, hold your horses, slow down, lets just take it easy! huh?

Your symphony is moving along at a nice clip, headed toward a magnificent crescendo when Reuben comes along. He slows the whole movement down. Frequently without malice, he impedes the forward movement of the enterprise. Note that he doesn't bring sounds to a halt— he only slows them down. When Reuben is around, we don't witness a work stoppage as much as a productivity decrease.

Reuben is alive and well whenever we see the team member that won't meet the project deadline or who waits until the last minute to verify facts and figures. Reuben is the pastor who defers a decision for no apparent reason while an enthusiastic committee awaits approval. Reuben is the teacher who insists all students learn at the same pace even though some have outdistanced their peers in reading rate and comprehension. Reuben is the art teacher insisting that first-graders draw inside the lines in their coloring books, while those children hunger for the abstract adventure outside the lines. Reuben is the worker who slows down the work in the name of quality control and conformity.

CHAPTER 7

Fred Fortissimo | N |

Every team has one. He's the loudmouth. Never one for being absorbed into the woodwork, he's seen and heard whenever possible. He's the overbearing one who heaps publicity upon himself and his doings. He'd never be accused of hiding his light under a bushel. A lover of the public display, he's the life of the party. Not given to quiet entrances, he announces his own arrival and expects to see excitement on the faces of his peers when he enters a room. Fred will see to it that your creative energies don't go unnoticed. He'll toot his horn *and* yours.

He keeps your finest work from getting buried in an ivory tower. Fred makes everything public. With Fred, there's always something to share with the rest of the world. He sees no need to wait until the "right moment" to reveal an idea. He wants to proclaim the news from the housetops.

The Freds must be held in check in your creativity context because their *volume* is more finely tuned than is their sense of *timing*. Sometimes you want to keep a lid on a project until the most appropriate disclosure time. With Fred around, that's extremely difficult . . . if not downright impossible.

Paula Pianissimo | P |

"Go placidly into the world," says one writer. That marks Paula. She is effective but not overwhelming. I used to think a musical passage wasn't effective unless it was blaring. In actuality, it is more difficult to control a soft passage. There can still be great intensity and expression in the pianissimo passage.

Paula is the person in our world who, without fanfare, gets the job done. She whispers while she works. Because she works quietly, it will be assumed by some that she's not pulling her weight. Paula is necessary for balance and texture in our creativity context.

Frequently the presence of Paula reminds us that all needn't be "out there" for everything to be well. In Matthew 6:5, Jesus instructs his hearers on the subject of prayer. He warns us that prayers should never be offered only to be heard by men. In our ministries and careers we run the risk of assuming that loud is good and soft is bad. There is great need for the quiet, understated elegance and industry of Paula Pianissimo.

You could go back through each of the preceding characters and turn each P into an N and vice versa. In fact, all positive people have some negative points and all negative people have some positive ones. When sizing up the workers in your circle of influence, look for both the P and the N. No person is all one or the other.

What is critical is that no one can eliminate our creative juices . . . but they *can* affect their flow. If you don't see anybody you know in the preceding list, create other characters. The goal is to get a handle on your silent and not so silent characters. It is unlikely that we will significantly change the people in our creativity context. Surely we will influence them and they us. As we begin or continue the adventure of innovation, our goal is not so much to bend our colleagues as to be aware of them.

As dangerous as throwing around labels might be, it is helpful to size up the folks around you. Every organization or ministry has a style. They have a preferred way of doing things. Sometimes that style is corporately held. At other times we see only the desires of one dominant character. Once you know what the preferred style is, the element of surprise, which wipes out so many folks, is greatly reduced.

For example, if the company is headed or controlled by a Steven Staccato type, there are some assumptions you may make. His style will influence the way he handles conflict and the way he handles you! There is no going off in a new and exciting direction until you acknowledge the prevailing "philosophy."

What is our course of action if we are surrounded by people who do not enhance what we do? Can we be our best innovative selves if our creativity context is swarming with those whose minds are closed? Certainly our best ideas are shaped as we bounce them off our fellow workers, but we're not limited to that. Let me offer a few suggestions for enhancing your generative skills even if your surroundings aren't creativity-friendly.

Corner Your Colleagues

Pick your colleagues' brains, observe their styles, get to know their likes and dislikes. Get beyond the cliches and seek to know what they think. It is always surprising for me to hear about people who have worked together in the same office for fifteen years and who have never met each other's spouses or families. In fact, they themselves haven't met apart from the job. How can you know what to expect in that creativity context if you don't know the players?

Certainly some people will only be your friends at work or in your places of ministry. The lines will be drawn and those folks will simply not move in your social circle. However, we cannot go on seeing people only at work or at our service organizations or at our churches and suggest that we know them well. A few meetings at the water cooler does not foster intimacy! If Jack affects my output, it is imperative that I spend time with him.

Supplement Your Surroundings

I talk much about your work/ministry context because we frequently spend half our waking hours in such settings. But sometimes nothing happens there that gets your engine running. Occasionally you will have to reach outside that sphere to get stimulated.

For instance, you may be in a very conservative company where innovation is squashed. Do you then dry up and die? No, you supplement! You go to other watering holes and derive sustenance, affirmation, and encouragement from them. You read, listen to tapes, go to seminars (even if you must bear the cost personally), and "hang out" with other creativity-minded folks. You seek elsewhere what you are not getting at your home base.

If your company dining room (or cafeteria) is full of clock-watching, pessimistic, complaining, whining malcontents, eat someplace else. If your Sunday school class is in a rut but you don't feel you can leave it, have a friend tape *his* class and commit yourself to listening to the tape later. One of the reasons business magazines do well is that people want to know what's happening in companies other than their own. Reading about others' benefit programs, policies, research and development, marketing strategies, and training programs supplements their knowledge of their own company. Christian leadership magazines, books, and tapes provide the same.

Raise Up a Model

That model needn't be you, but it *may* be. If you are trying to be creative in a pool of people going nowhere, give those people an alternative to emulate. Perhaps your fellows have not seen what you've seen, heard what you've heard. Push that article their way. Lend them that tape that inspired you. Take them to hear that outstanding speaker that excites you.

I recently met a young college student who was interested in writing. Wanting to chat about a mutual interest, I asked him if he were aware of a certain magazine for writers. His mother, who was part of our conversation, found a copy on the newsstand that week and gave her son a gift subscription. I enjoyed the simple pleasure of turning him to a helpful source of writing models.

Give them resources that will change and charge them. In the New Testament an older Christian named Paul took under his wing a young man named Timothy. Paul not only challenged Timothy to improve himself but he gave him an example: "What you heard from me, keep as the pattern of sound teaching, with faith and love in Christ Jesus" (2 Timothy 1:13).

Do you want your Reuben Rubatos to be less lethargic? Wish your Fanny Fermata would stop holding up your works? Provide a model. Be a pattern. We determine much of the temperature and texture of our creativity context. We often set the pace and invite others to follow, to keep up. We are surrounded but not overwhelmed!

MAYBE YOU SHOULDN'T CLEAN YOUR ROOM

 few years ago our local public broadcasting station aired an Oscar-nominated documentary about the late Isaac Bashevis Singer. Singer was a national treasure, one of the few remaining writers and protectors of Yiddish literature. Arriving in Brooklyn from his native Poland in 1935, Singer gave himself to writing stories that delight their readers. Curl up in your bed sometime and read some of his short stories. You will be richer and fuller when you put the book down.

Part of the documentary featured footage of Singer in his Manhattan apartment. As he stepped over books and papers in one very cluttered room, Singer explained, "If I clean up this room, it would lose its character. Before God said, 'Let there be light' there was chaos. So chaos is even older than the light." For the pack rats among us, that was a tremendously affirming statement.

The physical environment in which you create has a profound effect on your output. Let's look at your surroundings under three headings.

The Room Itself

Think of the place where you do most of your creating. Most of us will generate ideas in a variety of places, with insight arresting us as we drive, walk along, jog, swim, chat with co-workers in the hall, in the elevator, etc. However, there is usually a "command center" where it all comes together. It's the studio where you do your sculpting, the loft where you write, your office which contains the tools of your trade, and where the view inspires your best thoughts. It's the basement music room where you can play loudly without disturbing anyone and experiment with notes until that perfect melody comes. It is the library carrel which is, by now, your private hideaway. It is that park near your house that always invites your attention as you walk and which never fails to give you, in return, an energizing nugget with which to start your week.

Even if your special place is outdoors, you probably have an indoor spot in which you assemble the pieces of your creativity puzzle. Now consider your style of work. Are you a person who needs a blank piece of paper at the beginning of each task? Do you need to start off with a clean slate each day? Then you are probably the type that requires a clean desk or workstation. You are the person who tidies up each afternoon or evening before going home, because the thought of diving in tomorrow with today's stuff on the desk does not appeal to you. For you, a clean desk is a sign that you have completed today's tasks.

Others like the feeling of work always being in progress. They like a project to have that cumulative look. "Don't touch anything. Leave it like it is and tomorrow I'll pick up where I left off."

Both types must be true to themselves. Let the room reflect you and your preferred working style. Some work best if the room is stark and minimally decorated. Still others need posters, executive toys on the desk, and designer furniture, with diplomas, certificates, and plaques adorning the walls. Some require plenty of open space, providing ample room for pacing the floor. Their colleagues may want no spaces, but rather, a room in which each piece of furniture seems to kiss the others.

We commit the greatest crime when we endeavor to be what we're not. Creativity is seriously hampered when we deviate from our authentic selves. *Stop apologizing for your room. Remember the idea of Isaac Bashevis Singer: Chaos preceded creation.*

If the most innovative, exciting ideas to ever come forth from your brain are born in a cluttered room, don't clean it. If you are brought to the cutting edge of your field by a room that is as clean as a hospital operating room, don't allow clutter.

While I am always on the prowl for ideas, my office is my primary workplace. A large room that overlooks a pond, it is a pleasant place to spend uninterrupted hours reading and writing. I have a wall of bookshelves where my treasured friends wait for me to open them. In one corner are a chair and lamp. I call this my reading corner. It is there that I frequently sit, chasing some obscure footnote or reading an engaging chapter. My desk is a traditional one with a large surface, most of which is covered with mail and "I'm-going-to-take-a-look-at-that" reading material.

CHAPTER 8

My favorite part of the office, however, is another corner where my stand-up desk is. Nothing more than an artist's table that tilts, it is the place where I do most of my initial writing. Permanently poised there are a concordance, a hymnal, a pack of index cards, a yellow pad, and assorted pens and highlighting markers. For me, standing at that table is the best "work mode." For some of my associates, a desk is the only place to work. Which is the right way, the better way?

> If a desk is an extension of an individual's personality, then what is the absence of a desk? An extension of Geoffrey Holder's personality. Owning this conventional piece of office furniture would hinder his creativity. Says Holder, "I do my best work as I roam; a desk would force me to focus on trivial details. Besides, now that God in His infinite wisdom has given us the portable telephone, I'm no longer dependent on being tethered to a wall jack." He continues in affirmation of his perpetual flow of creative juices, "My desk is wherever I happen to be at a given moment," which more often than not is in a taxi that's whisking him and his much sought after oil paintings around town. Taxis have come to be playfully known as his "rolling desk."[1]

What You Hear as You Work

I know of writers who must have absolute silence when they write. Others need some noise before they can get any work going. A large percentage of students do their homework in front of a television, with headphones attached to their heads, or with a radio blaring. The purist will probably argue for a noise-free environment and say that serious academic or managerial work demands it. But that is one point of view.

What sounds do you like to hear when you are at your best? Waves lapping the shore? Jackhammers rhythmically pounding out a tune? Children laughing? The swish of cars on the highway? A few birds singing? Nothing? Instrumental music? Vocal music? Consider the suggestion that what you hear seeps in and affects your output. I recently heard the story of an overweight woman undergoing surgery. As the surgeons finished the procedure and she was beginning to come out of her anesthetized state, she heard them make a derogatory remark about her body as it lay on the table. That woman had a difficult recovery, as she was convinced her doctor did not respect or like her.

Mark Peltier couldn't quite articulate it, but he knew he thrived better in some office settings than in others. It was more than whether his desk faced a window. It was the entire environment that enveloped him. Through research, Peltier became familiar with positive affect (PA), an environmentally-induced mood shift. Tests conducted in Japan concluded that a lemon scent in the air conditioning system cut computer errors in half. Other research showed that wood scents relaxed workers; the smell of mint stimulated them; and a mixture of rosemary and lemon improved concentration. Mark Peltier took this information and developed a company, HomeOffice InVironments, Inc., which will market a desktop device which ionizes the air, emits a white noise to cover office sounds, and releases fragrances to affect the worker. Mark Peltier saw what many of us have seen, but saw it differently.

CHAPTER 8

Likewise, what you hear, even if it be sub- or unconscious, affects your productivity. Therefore, *watch* what you *hear!* As for me, I have been ruined by my training. Part of my formal musical education consisted of courses in Ear Training and Form and Analysis. Such courses forced us to listen to pieces of music and then dissect them. What is the dominant theme? In what sections does it recur? How many sections are in this symphony? In the fugue, does the second episode imitate the first? In the second movement of the concerto, what is the role of the string section?

Whether for good or evil, those courses made it impossible for me to have background music in my office. I do not, nor have I ever had, a radio in my office. I would be stopping to analyze the harmonic structure of the music and it would become disruptive.

Deliberately determine the sounds around you. *If you are what you eat, you are also what you hear.* A popular motivational speaker was talking to an audience about the power of words. He asked, "How many of you have heard people describe a child's second year as the 'terrible twos'?" Several hands went up. He then suggested that if a child thinks you perceive that year as terrible, that child will not disappoint you. "Why not," continued the speaker, "consider that year the 'terrific twos'?"

Are you living *down* to the negative input around you? Decide to live *up* to the affirming sounds with which you surround yourself. My wife has observed that I gravitate toward upbeat people whose eyes dance. I would never display rudeness toward a negative person, but neither would I choose to spend gobs of time with them. I am concerned that they might affect and infect me.

Is it possible that the sounds of your creativity work-place work against your best output? There is no need for paranoia here. Do not throw away your tape player or radio in an effort to "concentrate." In your mind, walk through your previous three days. How productive were they? If those days ended with your being satisfied, maybe you need not change a thing. On the other hand, perhaps you ended each day with a great sense of frustration. You didn't accomplish half of what you wanted to. What pro-hibited you? Too many sounds? Not enough? Let's not rule out the physical environment. The sights and sounds of your average day can stimulate or short circuit your cre-ativity.

What You Read

As I travel, I am regularly in the offices of leaders. I can usually tell, within a matter of minutes, whether the person is a reader. With that guess (which is almost always right) I can come to several other conclusions (which are also usually true). A woman or man who reads cannot help speaking about what they read. Without name-dropping for the sake of effect, they quite naturally refer to  those most recently discovered authors, trends, and ideas. They seem full of quotes and allusions. If it is true that we create out of the overflow of a full life, let us be on the prowl for new, fresh ideas. One source of such ideas is reading material. A few guidelines have helped me in my reading.

1. *Read regularly.*

At various times in my life I have taught piano. When my students were youngsters I would have eager mothers ask me how long their children should practice. My standard answer was that they should practice as long as they could concentrate. But whether they practiced fif teen minutes or one hour at a time, they should practice daily. Daily practice gets the piano piece "into the fingers." Fifteen minutes a day is better than a ninety minute cramming session on the day before the lesson.

When we are foraging for creativity fodder, we cannot afford to defer our reading until some "free day" when we will catch up. If you are reading a book (or two), plow through some of it (or them) today! Let that reading be done at the time of day when you are at your peak. Don't read first thing in the morning if you really would rather be going through your mail. Don't read late at night if you invariably fall off to sleep after a few paragraphs.

2. *Read widely.*

What's your chosen area of strength? What's your specialty? What are you good at? Who are the authors that affirm your biases and push your buttons? Forget all those answers for just a moment. Part of being highly creative is pushing ourselves into areas in which we are at a distinct disadvantage; areas in which the presuppositions are strange and unfamiliar; fields in which we don't know the names of the standard texts or leading authors; areas in which we cannot rattle off the latest statistics or make small talk with great confidence.

While this can be threatening, it is also very life-giving. The moment we step outside that environment in which we are most at home, we are introduced to an entirely new set of variables. Maybe you don't wish to subscribe to it, but purchase, just this month, a magazine about mechanical engineering, science, or animals. Ask a friend for the trade magazine from her field. Scour the sections of the newspaper which you would not normally read.

The best section of the Sunday *New York Times*, in my opinion, is the Book Review section. It contains a thorough review of what's new in the publishing world. You can subscribe to that section and regularly keep those good leads coming to your doorstep. If you often read novels, read non-fiction the next time around. *Diversity stimulates creativity.*

As part of your weekly routine, why not go to a newsstand and browse? Choose one publication you would only buy if you were trying to be creative! Buy that out-of-town newspaper to see what people are doing in other cities. Read whole books, short chapters, articles, paragraphs, footnotes, and anything else you can get your hands on.

3. *Capture what you read.*

Relax. I am not about to launch into a diatribe about elaborate filing systems and their value. Personally, I have not given myself to one. However, all the goodies we collect that will feed our creativity stream will be useless if we have no way to retrieve them at will.

With the advent of the personal computer in notebook, laptop, and desk models, you may choose to enter data on a disk and save it. You may opt for index cards filed under appropriate headings. When I was in graduate school I had a professor who looked at our class one day and essentially said, "Ladies and gentlemen, as you are reading, you will come across many quotes you will want to save. You will hear, in your travels, quotes you will want to remember. You may even put them on a scrap of paper, but you won't know where to find the scrap after a while. I suggest you carry a little book with you at all times. In it, simply record those things you read, conclude, or overhear. Then when you need it you will know where to find it." He then made the keeping of such a book an assignment for the semester.

It was such a valuable discipline that I have continued the practice all these years. So much do I want to be held accountable for always having that book with me, that I have offered audiences around the country a monetary reward on the spot, if they ever catch me without my "little black book."

In it I put words that strike me, stories that would make a gripping illustration, statistics that would liven up a presentation, the background story of a well-known person or object, jokes. When I need that fresh touch, that compelling angle, I needn't look far.

If you enjoyed that article you just read, what are you going to do about it? Even if you vigorously underline paragraphs throughout the book, take a few minutes and write the page numbers of outstanding passages in the front of the book. Those passages are then more easily retrieved.

Once you make the commitment to be an innovator, to be a "creator," there is no turning back. The process of exposing ourselves to new ideas, implementing those ideas, evaluating the implementation, and building a creativity memory bank, is a continuous process. Take control of your environment and see to it that it responds to your needs as a creative person. Paint the walls, clear the desk, buy a radio, or throw one out. Just get moving! You *are* what surrounds you.

Note

1. *Upscale Magazine*, June/July 1990, 15.

CHAPTER 9
IDEAS: WHERE TO FIND THEM

IDEAS: WHERE TO FIND THEM

ccasionally I have inadvertently thrown a piece of paper into a garbage can and have had to dig into the trash to retrieve it. I've always felt unclean doing so and always hoped nobody I knew would catch me so visibly ruining my image. For an idea, however—for an idea, I would enthusiastically dig in dirt!

Once we've become creativity-conscious, our goal is to get information, ideas. A change of mindset and approach is necessary here. Some think ideas are collected and compiled in cute books of illustrations, jokes for after-dinner speakers, toastmaster's  guides, and success stories. While these anthologies may help, you will be critically hampered if limited thereto. Ideas are literally all around us. In this brief chapter I want to show you *where* and *how* to find ideas that will feed your creativity machine and keep it running. My five favorite places/settings for ideas are:

1. *Newspapers, magazines, and books.*

At least a couple of times a week, if not daily, comb through newspapers and magazines. At a local stationery store, you can purchase a tool specifically designed for clipping articles. I carry such a tool with me at all times. Clip any article that strikes you. I immediately write an application or an idea in the margin of the article. This reminds me what it was that grabbed me as I first read it. Of course, I may see some other applications as I read it again.

Newspapers are full of goodies. Don't assume they are always in the same place. Some days, profound insights and ideas come to you from the comic page. Other days you will find yourself laughing or crying as you read the advice column. Have you ever read the "personals" section? Don't forget the sports pages. Frequently a tale of triumph, tragedy, determination, or budding potential awaits you there. The editorial pages grapple with "hot topics" in a way that puts new angles on those topics, thus opening up wide vistas for us readers. We throw away dozens of ideas every time we discard a newspaper or magazine.

Recently asked if I were selling any of my books, I replied that I was too young to dismantle my library. Your books, while not as easily culled as a magazine, hold worlds of thought in their pages. In the front of some books, I jot down a few page numbers that struck me during my first reading of the book. Those notes help guide me through either a second reading or a search for "the right illustration."

The pack rats among us could, in an effort to harness their ideas, save every periodical and book. Allow realism to take over here. You'll never read all the articles. You will never go back to that stack of back issues and pore over them . . . not even in your retirement. That being true, regularly do some gleaning and clipping. Trust your library skills to enable you, at a later time, to get at those goodies you may miss.

I always have, in my car, what I call a "light and line book." These are short, not-so-weighty, paperbacks that I want to read. I can usually breeze through them while standing in line or driving through a congested area. At every traffic light, I whip the book out and read a couple of lines. I have actually finished reading some pieces using this method. A magazine would also work well in that spot. I read when I am in the barber's chair or waiting for a plane. Or while in line at the supermarket. Why not? Unless you need those times for non-structured thinking (which is certainly valuable), why not turn it into reading time?

2. Nature.

In the natural objects and critters that dot the canvas of our world, we have a wealth of ideas. Watch three kittens chase a ball of yarn around for fifteen minutes and then think about your impending deadline. Did you get any ideas watching those kinetic wads of fur? What does the gentle lapping of water against rock do for you? Does it open your mind to some new angles?

Bishop William Robinson is the pastor of the Garden of Prayer Church of God in Christ in the Bronx, New York. Right in the middle of a less-than-tranquil area, he designed a sanctuary that brought the garden theme indoors. He brought together flowing water, greenery, rocks, and a picture of a Christ figure in prayer to create a beautiful diorama that creates a mood for the worshiper. There in the front of the worship space is a garden. Where did he dream that up? I suspect the inspiration came from nature.

> *The Problem:* Potato chips take up too much space in warehouses and on supermarket shelves, but they crumble when packed too tightly.
>
> *The Goal:* To pack, ship and sell them more compactly without crushing them.
>
> *The Solution:* According to industry legend, it went something like this: Forget about potato chips. Think about nature. What reminds you of potato chips? Leaves, of course, at least dry ones. They fall in various shapes, and when you press them together they crumble, just like potato chips. But wait! Wet leaves pack together tightly without crumbling. Suppose we moisten potato chips first and form them into some uniform shape? They could then be stacked and packed together tightly when dry. The result was *Pringles*, a landmark in food packaging though a dubious culinary achievement.[1]

Nature is replete with visual stimuli to help get your fountain flowing, your wheels spinning, your engine revved, your bearings oiled, your hair standing on end, and your tires out of the mud. The Center for Christian Leadership in Dallas has, as its logo, a flock of Canadian

Geese flying in formation. Their choice was made as a result of a study which suggested that geese flying in formation are more efficient than those who fly solo. A significant part of this center's philosophy of leadership training has been shaped by a natural phenomenon. When you walk in parks, fields, and botanical gardens, what do you see? Elizabeth Barrett Browning has written:

> Earth's crammed with fire and every common
> bush
> afire with God.
> But only he who sees takes off his shoes
> The rest sit 'round it and pluck blackberries.[2]

As our creativity muscle begins to flex itself more and more, we are less and less willing to let anything pass us by. Occasionally, just for the fun of it, choose a setting and see how many practical observations you can pull out of it. Make the connections that serve you. Perhaps skipping rocks across a pond reminds you of the nature of written reports. You can get several good bounces out of it before it sinks. I bragged to a friend that, in an effort to force myself to be fresh, I'd discarded several years of notes and speeches I'd written. He introduced me to the concept of "cannibalizing" one's own work. That is, we use it, rework it, and use it again. A rock skipping on the surface of a pond reminds me of that concept.

Can you get another skip out of that project on which you worked so hard and long? What do you see when you go white-water rafting or spelunking or swimming or jogging or walking or fishing? What do you see when you are simply outdoors enjoying it all? Have your dictation machine or your little black book ready, because if you will open up even a little, ideas will come!

3. *Children.*

If you have no contact with children you are to be pitied. If you are childless or your children are grown and you have no grandchildren, volunteer some time to a Sunday school class, an elementary school, a community center, or a neighbor. Some gems only and always fall from lips which have been flapping for seven years or less.

At the time I am writing this book, I have no children of my own, but I have always been around children. Having siblings significantly younger than I, during some of my growing up years I functioned like a teenage father. In addition, I have young nieces, nephews, and friends' children who provide me a never-ending source of material.

One youngster who has captured my heart was watching his mother bathe his younger brother. Mommy said, "Nathan, close the door so the draft won't get on Philip." Days later, Nathan himself was in the bathroom. As his mother opened the door he asked, "Please close the door, so the giraffes won't get on me." I thought about the "thing" we've never seen, called a draft. How does that connect with something we've seen, such as a giraffe? Maybe they don't connect at all. Perhaps a creative parent could give "unvisible" objects, like drafts, names. An energy conservation program could be launched in the home with signs such as, "Let's keep giraffes out of our house. Don't forget to close the door tightly when you come in." A picture of a giraffe could be the centerpiece of the poster.

IDEAS: WHERE TO FIND THEM

As a child, my youngest sister asked my mother, "Did God ever die?" After my mother said no, Roslyn went on to ask, "Did Jesus ever die?" After hearing yes, Roslyn paused a few seconds, then said, "I'm sticking with God."

As I have been sorting out the issues of life that matter, I have been reminded that even a child wants to stick with the One who will not suffer death. What an insight into the understanding of death. Even a youngster sees death as the Great Interrupter.

Now, understand, we never spend time with children *in order to* get ideas. However, if you will spend significant time with children, you will always come away with ideas. As part of the research for this chapter, I visited a kindergarten class at the Byfield School in Byfield, Massachusetts. What a time we had! I was reminded of the wonder of a child's mind. That mind has not yet become cluttered with the barriers of logic or caution.

I took with me a box filled with ordinary items from around the house and asked those five- and six-year-old visionaries to tell me what those items could be used for, other than their "intended purpose." The box contained three sponge balls (which became eyes, a hat, a juggler's tools, covers for a bun in a girl's hair, and a nose for a clown), a Frisbee (which became a plate, a hat), and a wooden coat hanger without the crossbar (which became a boomerang). A rattan trivet became a plate, a hat, a Frisbee, a large cookie; paired with a sponge ball, an ice cream scoop became a small lacrosse set, a golf ball holder; the brush attachment for a vacuum cleaner became a microphone; the pole-like handle of a manual carpet sweeper became a baton.

Edwin Land was at the beach with his young daughter. After he took her picture with a simple camera, she asked when she could see it. Land replied that the film had to be developed first. His daughter asked, "Why can't we see the pictures now?" That question inspired Land to invent the instant photography technology we associate with the Polaroid Land camera.

After we spent several minutes with the box of goodies, we turned our attention to items of clothing. "What else could you do with your shoe if it became too small for you?" Among the answers: Use it as a boat; as a catcher's mitt; golfers could lay it on its side, take out their putters, and use it as a golf ball cup. To the question, "What could you do with shoelaces?" my young charges replied: Use them as belts, bracelets, necklaces, lifelines to drowning people, and jump ropes. What could we do with clumps of hair? One youngster blurted out, "Tie it onto the end of a stick and make a broom."

I almost felt like a traitor walking away from those bright minds. I know that, given time and a traditional approach to education, many of them will not have their creativity muscle affirmed, challenged, and stretched. It will be repressed in favor of the "greater goal" of memorizing facts, seeing everything in its "proper context," and regurgitating trivia for meaningless exams and academic exercises. I walked away knowing that the joy of seeing multiple uses of ordinary objects would serve them well in the "real" world, but not in the standard kindergarten curriculum. My host teacher, Angela Wright, is a bright, inventive, energized teacher who allows the children much time and space to explore . . . to dream . . . to be. I hope her style of teaching is much more the norm and less the exception to the rule.

4. *Hobbies.*

What do you do when you're not "on" and what ideas may you get from those hobbies or leisure time activities? Does your gardening offer a model for some project at work, church, or synagogue? When you are rehabilitating an old house or building something in a basement shop or firing a vase in the kiln, what connections do you make? The parable and paradigms are there, but not always so easily seen.

Let's suppose your hobby is tennis. Every chance you get, you are on the court either playing or practicing. You eat, sleep, walk, talk tennis. Your hobby consumes you and you decide that since this is true, you should at least profit by its spilling over into your company. You decide to use a little tennis strategy for your next staff meeting. While it is

fun to play doubles, you've discovered that you like playing singles much more, because then you don't have to share your side of the court with anybody. You like all the action for yourself.

Hey, wait a minute! Isn't that exactly what's happening with the marketing division? Isn't Stan refusing to share the court with Susan? Isn't he hogging all the fresh leads, making it difficult for her to get a hit? Is she having a hard time returning the few serves that come her way because Stan is all over the court? Eureka! Your hobby has given you not only an analogy, but an idea. Now let it inform the way you deal with your staff members at the next meeting. There is no rule written that says hobbies must provide respite only. They may also provide insight (even if there was such a rule, you and I would at least challenge it!).

5. Observation.

Most of us have been introduced to the sport of people-watching. More than a sport, it is an art.

IDEAS: WHERE TO FIND THEM

Commonplace is the person who can sit in an airline terminal and stare at people for a couple of hours. Ordinary is the chap who can, while eating pancakes at a local restaurant, overhear the conversation of the breakfast party at the next table. But rare is the person who knows what to do with the info. Make it work for you!

When you observe a pattern, an idiosyncrasy, a humorous event . . . record it. Write about it; reflect on it; connect it; work it. Turn your attention to the most pressing project facing you. Now rehearse, in your mind, the last setting in which you did some observing. Any bridges between the two? Maybe so, maybe not. But you cannot afford to skip the opportunity to investigate.

My late grandfather called my grandmother "Bob" for much of their married life. As her name is Rebecca, the way Pop got to "Bob" wasn't clear to me. On one of the many occasions on which I pumped him for familial tidbits, I asked him why he called Grandma, Bob. Pop then told me about a couple he knew when he was single. He'd observed their marriage and admired it. The husband in that couple called his wife Bob. Pop determined that when he married, he would call his wife Bob with the hope that their marriage would be as fine as that of the couple he'd observed. (By the way, at the time of Pop's death, he and "Bob" had been married for sixty-three years. It was the best marriage I have ever seen, with no exceptions.)

What are you moved to do, to try, to think about, as a result of what you've seen? To conclude this chapter I am going to walk you through a paragraph from a recent *Boston Globe* article. Let's read it and see if we can generate a minimum of six ideas from it. The article is a profile of jazz pianist Dave Brubeck.

> As a boy growing up on a ranch in California, Brubeck sang to the gait of the horse he was riding and to the sound of an engine pumping water to irrigate the crops. He heard rhythm in the honking of car horns and in the rumble of trains. He still does . . . "To improvise [Brubeck said], you have to be angry and frustrated. Anger is a very important emotion. Through improvisation, a jazz musician can voice that anger. Jazz is protest. It's an art form in which extemporaneous feelings are expressed. Improvisation involves letting loose your feelings."[3]

With just this brief excerpt, we can generate scores of ideas. Let's strive for fluency *and* flexibility as we react to the paragraph.

1. We sometimes use anger and frustration as synonyms. What is the difference between the two? This could serve as a piece of "fun" or "beneficial" research. What practicing psychologists do I know? What would they say about this? Have I often been frustrated and called it anger?

2. I will return to the forgotten musical instrument of my youth. Why couldn't I get beyond the printed page with that thing? Why was I so bound? Why couldn't I "jam" in those "jam sessions" we had after school? Was it because I lacked anger?

3. Let's go to a nearby stable and ask permission to

record a horse walking or galloping. Take the recording to a musician, to be transcribed. What does a horse's gallop look like on paper? Is there a song that comes to mind as I see and hear that rhythmic pattern?

4. If we didn't have music, how might we vent our anger? I think I will examine what kind of music I and my family listen to. Is it the music of anger or does it soothe us? What are the precise elements of music that excite, that incite? The teenagers in the family will be asked to "defend" their choices of music, from an emotional point of view. What does this contribute to your serenity or the lack thereof?

5. If I were to describe my company or church using musical imagery, would I see any jazz in it at all? Is there room for improvisation among us? Do we find it easy or acceptable to "let loose our feelings?"

6. There is something I do with the same regularity with which the boy Brubeck rode horses. What is that thing? Could it offer insights that I have overlooked? Have I become deaf to the horse's gait, the engine's pump, the honking of the horn, and rumble of the trains? Let me reexamine my mundane tasks.

The article is longer, offering plenty of other departure points. Had we more time, we could dissect every line. Preacher, do you see a series on anger in Brubeck's quote? Are you a music teacher? Did you ever think of teaching rhythm to your students by taking them to the zoo? Ideas are literally everywhere.

As I was writing this chapter I received a call from a desperate student who needs to earn $600 in a week. Given this unexpected bill she must pay and the shortness of the time, there were options that could not be considered. However, we generated a few good ideas on the phone in about fifteen minutes. We grabbed the ideas out of the air. They were right around us. "What skills do you have that you could offer to people?" I asked. "Who do you know who would be willing to pay in advance for services you could render later, or over a period of time? What assets do you have that you could sell? What neighbors would give you items from their basement that you could then sell at a flea market or garage sale?" If we'd had more hours, we could have dreamed up dozens of additional ideas.

Join Me in the Gym

Imagine that your mind is a muscle. It must be exercised. We cannot simply allow our idea-generating facility to atrophy and then wonder why we are not more creative. We must play games, take on the brain teasers, endure the riddles told us by our children (and thereby learn something), filter through the reams of paper that come across our desks each year and never, ever stop digging around for "stuff." As in physical exercise, the waking up of a dormant mental muscle can be painful. The pain of those first stretches is not to be compared to the glory and thrill of finding freshness. Decide now that you will endure the pain, for the gain; that you will pay whatever price creativity will exact from you.

IDEAS...WHERE TO FIND THEM

Notes

    1. "Imagination to Go," *Psychology Today*, May 1984, 48.

    2. Elizabeth Barrett Browning, "Aurora Leigh," *Aurora Leigh and Other Poems* (London: Women's Press, 1978).

    3. "Brubeck's jazz: music of anger, music of joy," Boston Globe, 3 June 1990, B48.

THE PIGGYBACK PRINCIPLE

THE PIGGYBACK PRINCIPLE

n the days before pipe organs were powered by large, efficient motors, air was pumped into the pipes manually. By constantly working the bellows, a young, energetic man or woman would serve the great virtuosos of the era by being their pumpers.

A very talented and arrogant (why do those terms so frequently get paired?) organ master gave a concert to a standing-room-only crowd. To thunderous applause he left the stage for the intermission.

"That was some first half we gave them, wasn't it?" asked the enthusiastic, tired young bellowman.

"We?" queried the maestro. "We? I am the performer here. They were applauding me. I practiced, I gave the moving interpretation of the pieces. You simply pump the air!"

The bellowman sheepishly nodded. When the second half of the concert began, the organist strutted out onto the stage. With flair he sat down at the keyboard, arched his arms and brought them down with great drama. There was no sound. Embarrassed, he brought himself up to his full height, cleared his throat, glared around the console to his pumper and struck the keys again. Silence. "Air, give me air!" he whispered. The lad peeked around the console and said, "Shall it be *we*, then?"

There is rarely a project, task, vision, concept, dream, idea, or accomplishment for which you may legitimately take full credit. There is always someone (or, most often, there are someones) who share the glory with you. While you might get the public adulation and praise, there were people in the shadows who were so committed to you or the task, that they gave themselves. For every great organist, there is a pumper!

Too ancient an illustration? All right—for every successful student there is a supportive parent, guardian, sibling, best friend. For every rising executive there is a supervisor who believes in that man or woman.

There is an administrative assistant who wants you to succeed. For every inventor there is a housekeeper who throws food under the door so you can work well into the wee hours. For every writer there is a person who keeps the phone from ringing and protects those precious writing hours. Those often nameless helpers deserve the applause. They ought to be on stage with us. Without their air, our pipes could not produce the glorious sounds of which they are capable.

More often than generating wonderful ideas and developing them on our own, we are *piggybacking* on the concepts of another. This stacking of one idea upon another is given several names. Some call it *enlarging*. One articulates an idea. Another person in the group enlarges upon it by adding an angle, and so on. Other writers in the field of creative thinking call this technique the *stepping stone*. One idea leads to another. My colleague's flash of insight serves as a springboard for my own contribution. I have also heard it called *plusing*. You speak and your fellow innovator says, "Plus . . ." and he adds a piece. Across the table a colleague chimes in with, "And something else we could do is . . ." A few minutes later, one cries out, "Okay, suppose we try it this way . . ." The possibilities are endless when you take one idea and piggyback on it. I like to think of the idea as a solid object. What are some things I could do to it? I could:

1. Cut it up
2. Shrink it
3. Paint it
4. Squeeze it
5. Bake it
6. Enlarge it
7. Rearrange its pieces
8. Put Tabasco Sauce on it
9. Poke it with a screwdriver
10. Put it in a blender
11. Freeze it
. . . and a thousand other processes.

Now, take your idea. What would happen if we "froze it?" How would it (or we) change if we "spiced it up?" This is, I admit, a bit weird. This is a foray into abstract thinking. If my idea is bland, I might apply number 8 and "put some fire into it." I am not even sure what that means for you, but you know when spice is lacking! I might sense that I am not working closely enough with my colleagues. In that case, apply number 10. Perhaps I am rushing the project. Enter number 11, as I freeze my idea in time and let it stand as is for awhile. You could take any one of these items and call it something else. That is precisely the point. See it differently! If picturing a problem or an idea as a solid object helps you, then do it.

An illustration would be fun to work through right here:

Idea: Your company wants to do something different in place of the annual picnic for employees and their families. Let's eavesdrop on the meeting of the Picnic Planning Committee (the name of the committee alone is enough to make you want to go someplace else that weekend!). I'll comment on the meeting as we go along.

FRAN: I have the notes that Ellen gave me on last year's picnic.

HERBERT: Let's see them.

DONNA: Why don't we do something completely different? (Number 9—Donna's poking around with a screwdriver. Anything alive here? Anything about this picnic worth saving?)

JIM: Yeah, let's have the picnic in the Bahamas. (Number 6-Let's enlarge it. Think big.)

FRAN: We probably can't do the Bahamas, but how about a sunnier spot than last year?

(Number 10—Let me mix my concerns with Jim's.)

HERBERT: The problem last year wasn't the spot; it's the time of year. We can't always count on good, hot weather in May. (Numbers 1 and 2— Let's isolate the problem and see it in bite-sized pieces. The problem may be smaller than we thought.)

DONNA: Let's look at a date change. Maybe we could go with something in June. (Number 7— Let's rearrange the date, not necessarily the event.)

FRAN: When do most of the kids get out of school?

JIM: That won't matter if we go with a Saturday instead of the Memorial Day Monday.

HERBERT: I heard some complaints last year that the event was too long. How about starting later to give us a chance to sleep late that Saturday?

DONNA: I'm all for that. Saturday's the only day I get to snooze a little.

JIM: Let's go back to Fran's idea about another spot. Has anyone been to Slater Park in Bridgeton? They have great facilities there. (A silence follows.) All right. Why don't we have our meeting there next week and look it over? (Number 10— Jim blends his thoughts with Fran's.)

FRAN: So far we've talked about changing the month, the day, the place, and the length of the picnic. The folks won't even recognize the picnic when we get finished with it. (All of the above—The group considers doing something to the idea, to change the way it looks altogether.)

DONNA: Good!

In this short, rather typical meeting, we have seen piggybacking in a practical form. Note that the members of the committee did not pour cold water on each idea. They simply listened and added to the idea as they felt comfortable doing so. Actually, what you just read was the opposite of what I call the "salami meeting." In those, the participants slice each other's ideas and conclude with several pieces all over the table. In a piggybacking session, we all bring our slices to the table and emerge with a whole.

It is crucial that we avoid the tendency to assign value to these styles. One creative thinking technique is not better than another. They are simply different. Meetings will not always be as smooth as this example. However, when a group of "creators" gets together and decides to do something more than defend a position, there are exciting other ideas that will emerge. There is a great temptation to play "Can you top this?" with idea generation. The game becomes one of contributing a "better" idea.

But with piggybacking, the goal is not to "ace" your committee mate. The aim is, rather, to enhance his/her idea. The group plays with one idea and comes up with variation after variation. In the previous example, the subject of discussion is the picnic, period. Note how every comment has to do with that event.

Often our meetings are so uncontrolled that they hit too many subjects in a given time. As desirable as that is on some occasions (for instance, in a brainstorming session), it is death to a piggybacking session. In such a meeting, there is one central topic. The question then becomes "what can we do to this idea? Can we add to it? Subtract from it? Divide it? Multiply it? Slow it down? Speed it up? Move it decidedly forward? Move it backward?"

Word association is a form of piggybacking in that it stays with one "starter word" and generates as many associated words as the group can stand. There are at least two forms of the word association exercise. One is the form in which each participant suggests a word associated with the *last word* uttered. The other is an exercise in which each participant continues to associate with the *first word* uttered. Even then, with enough freedom, the group members will gain distance from the problem. Returning to the company picnic problem, the

Alan Witten thought that if doctors could "see" babies in the womb through ultrasound technology, that same technology could be applied in other fields. Witten drilled four-inch wide holes twenty feet into the ground and fired a shotgun into the ground, recording the noise patterns on underground microphones. Witten's technique— Geophysical Diffraction Tomography (GDT)—will have applications ranging from archaeological digs to finding illegally buried toxic waste. Many people were aware of ultrasound, but Witten saw it differently.

word association version of piggybacking might look like this:

PICNIC
food
bugs
games
cars
canoes
children
adults
senior citizens
drinks
grass
lakes
barbecue grills
charcoal
ice chests
bathing suits

We could take any one of these items and develop it, using a brainstorming approach. But with the piggyback version of word association we must stay with the picnic idea (the other version would allow you to go off on a tangent and discuss *kinds* of lakes, *colors* of bathing suits, etc.).

For some, this seems unnecessarily limiting. To them, creativity is that exercise or frame of mind that knows no limit. I am indebted to Rollo May, who in his book *Courage to Create* suggests that creativity, by its very nature, has limits. Says May, ". . . limits are not only unavoidable in human life, they are also valuable . . .

creativity itself requires limits, for the creative act arises out of the struggle of human beings with and against that which limits them."[1]

May goes on to list death, sickness, neurological, and metaphysical limits as those which are ever-present. The

creative person does not have the luxury of thinking that "the sky is the limit." One of the great truths which informs our idea-generating exercises is that we are mortal. We are in a physical body with certain boundaries.

CHAPTER 10

We are in a certain geographical area that may or may not offer particular resources.

While this could sound disappointing (especially for the dreamer/visionary) it is not intended to dissuade you. With all that is in you, go for it! Simply be aware that whether we are associating with words, people, or ideas, there are boundaries. It is to be hoped that those boundaries are large, welcoming the adventurous ones and bidding them, "Come and create."

Edward De Bono, in his book *Six Thinking Hats*, talks about the backward and forward effects of an idea.

> In normal thinking we use judgment. How does this idea compare to what I know? How does this idea compare to my established patterns of experience? We judge that it does not fit or we point out why it does not fit. . . . We may call this the *backward effect* of an idea. We look backwards at our past experience to assess the idea.[2]

De Bono then proceeds to suggest another way of thinking, in which judgment is replaced by movement.

> I want to make it absolutely clear that movement is not just an absence of judgment. Many early approaches to creative thinking talk about deferring, suspending, or delaying judgment. I think this is much too weak, because it does not tell the thinker what to do—only what not to do.
>
> . . . with movement we use an idea for its *forward effect*. We use an idea to see where it will

get us. We use an idea to see what it will lead to. In effect we use an idea to move forward.[3]

In a piggybacking session we keep moving forward with the idea until its advance yields usable, new ideas.

Piggyback on the idea that no choir members should wear robes. What other ideas are generated as you discuss that idea?

Try these others:

- All persons in our company will be given a 40 percent raise this year.

- No children are permitted in the church office.

- Only our employees earning less than $35,000 a year will be given a company-paid life insurance policy.

- *Every deacon in our congregation will be asked to give pastoral oversight to fifteen to twenty families.*

- *My next car will be of foreign make.*

- *My next car will be "previously owned."*

- *No couple in the world should be permitted to have more than five children.*

Try these starter statements with some friends. There are no right answers. In fact, you may not generate answers at all. You may emerge from your session with a greater appreciation of your company's benefits program or the world population crisis.

❖

The prophet Isaiah describes the message of ancient Scripture as "Precept upon precept, line upon line, here a little, there a little" (Isaiah 28:10, KJV). Growing up I heard godly old men and women pray, countless times, ". . . and lead us from one good degree of grace to another."

In piggybacking, we stack idea upon idea, flash of light upon flash of light—and in so doing, we are led from one degree of creativity to another.

Notes

1. Rollo May, *Courage to Create* (New York: Bantam Books, 1984), 134-135.
2. Edward De Bono, *Six Thinking Hats* (Boston: Little, Brown and Company, 1985), 143-144.
3. Ibid.

WHAT'S STOPPING YOU?

f we would listen to the gurus of the Positive Thinking movement, all we need do to succeed is to think optimistically. If we would set goals and believe that we will reach them, we shall prosper. If we will plan our work, then work our plan, nothing can stop us. This is standard rhetoric for the movement. However, it is far too simplistic a view.

There are not only imagined barriers to our productivity and to our ability to be creative—there are real, tangible roadblocks that confront us. They cannot be eradicated merely by articulating them. We must confront those walls and work diligently to tear them down.

The call to creativity is at once a rational and irrational call. While we must give ourselves to clear thinking that is purposeful and logical, on the other hand, there are surprises ahead for which we could not have planned. When we investigate the reasons we are not more creative, we find there are logical and illogical reasons. Handling the barriers is one of the foundational and ongoing tasks of the creative person.

Most of us are adept at rattling off alleged reasons, but frequently our list is full of scapegoats, not barriers. We are looking for someone to blame rather than something to face. The most creative people are so intentional that they will let nothing and no one stop them from their pursuit. I urge you to take on these suggested barriers and the ones that appear only on your list. See this list as a beginning. Add to it. Argue with it. Then, after all is said and done, see to it that more is done than said.

CHAPTER 11

1. *Fear.*

The cost of being a renegade may be too high for some of us. That fear may take many forms—fear of being labeled rebel, radical, young upstart, troublemaker. If we are challenging the rule—written or set in place by a revered founder of an organization—we might fear being seen as an ingrate. The simple fear of failure might be enough to paralyze us. Suppose my bright ideas flop? Will I be given another chance? Will I be the Edsel of the season, remembered only for my failure? Oddly enough, some are afraid they will succeed. If I am successful at my creative venture, will I be expected to produce another great idea and then another? If I am not certain I can keep turning out the hits, I may choose not to create at all.

This may have stopped the potential investor described in one of Jesus' parables:

> Therefore keep watch, because you do not know the day or the hour. Again, it will be like a man going on a journey, who called his servants and entrusted his property to them. To one he gave five talents of money, to another two talents, and to another one talent, each according to his ability. Then he went on his journey. The man who had received the five talents went at once and put his money to work and gained five more. So also, the one with the two talents gained two more. But the man who had received the one talent went off, dug a hole in the ground and hid his master's money. After

a long time the master of those servants returned and settled accounts with them. The man who had received the five talents brought the other five. "Master," he said, "you entrusted me with five talents. See, I have gained five more." His master replied, "Well done, good and faithful servant! You have been faithful with a few things; I will put you in charge of many things. Come and share your master's happiness!" The man with the two talents also came. "Master," he said, "you entrusted me with two talents; see, I have gained two more." His master replied, "Well done, good and faithful servant! You have been faithful with a few things; I will put you in charge of many things. Come and share your master's happiness!" Then the man who had received the one talent came. "Master," he said, "I knew that you are a hard man, harvesting where you have not sown and gathering where you have not scattered seed. So I was afraid and went out and hid your talent in the ground. See, here is what belongs to you." His master replied, "You wicked, lazy servant! So you knew that I harvest where I have not sown and gather where I have not scattered seed? Well then, you should have put my money on deposit with the bankers, so that when I returned I would have received it back with interest. Take the talent from him and give it to the one who has the ten talents" (Matthew 25:13-28).

CHAPTER 11

Might this man's fear (v. 25) have been of both success and failure? If he invested poorly, his master would be angry. If he invested wisely, perhaps he'd be given a larger amount and be expected to repeat his outstanding performance. Much has been written about the fear of failure. When touched by fear, I think of the worst possible outcome, respond to that imaginary scenario, and move on. Having dealt with the very worst case, I am free to operate effectively.

Imagine that you have the responsibility of planning this summer's Vacation Bible School at your church. Let's go through a worst-case scenario:

- You don't get enough teachers.

- The curriculum you ordered months in advance doesn't arrive.

- Despite ample publicity, only six children show up for a ten-day program.

- The weather is terrible and all your outdoor activities have to be canceled.

Enough! Enough! Now, be creative. See the situation differently. Make something orderly out of this mess! If you will do that with the hypothetical scenario, you will be freed from your fear in the actual planning stage. Many of the monsters we fear, never appear. But what if they do? Answer *that* question and you are free.

2. *It ain't broke.*

A pastor I know had been elected to the presidency of a Christian organization. As there was also a full-time executive director, the president's role was minimal and more public-relations oriented and annual conference-connected than it was administrative. Several denominations have such configurations. Although he wouldn't be making earth-shattering policy changes in his tenure, I was disappointed when he told me his philosophy of ministry has always been, "If it ain't broke, don't fix it." He

spent his two-year term as a "maintenance man." The perception that a church, organization, or company is "holding its own" is "competent" or "isn't interested in changing" stifles the creativity of many. We see creative solutions not because something doesn't work, but because it can be better, fresher, more relevant.

On one occasion a young man approached Jesus and presented his "if it ain't broke" self to the master. From all appearances, the man was doing better than all right. He wasn't merely surviving, he was thriving. Jesus saw him differently and offered him a better life. As our master saw him, he needed fixing.

> As Jesus started on his way, a man ran up to him and fell on his knees before him. "Good teacher," he asked, "what must I do to inherit eternal life?" "Why do you call me good?" Jesus answered. "No one is good—except God alone. You know the commandments: 'Do not murder, do not commit adultery, do not steal, do not give false testimony, do not defraud, honor your father and mother.' " "Teacher," he declared, "all these I have kept since I was a boy." Jesus looked at him and loved him. "One thing you lack," he said. "Go, sell everything you have and give to the poor, and you will have treasure in heaven. Then come, follow me." At this, the man's face fell. He went away sad, because he had great wealth (Mark 10:17-22).

The account in Mark is my favorite because only Mark tells us that the young man ran to Jesus and knelt before him (v. 17). Only Mark tells us that Jesus gave the young executive a look of love (v. 21, cf. Matthew 19:16-30, Luke 18:18-30). This guy wasn't all that bad. He was far more law-abiding, commandment-keeping, and upstanding than most people I know . . . and he was proud of it! Imagine the confidence with which he uttered verse 20. It is the Christ, who is not a maintenance man, who says, "One thing you lack."

What is lacking in *your* ministry? Be not satisfied with, "It's going OK." Maybe it ain't broke—but it's quite broken down! That's reason enough to hold it to the light, cause enough to dissect it. This is a compelling reason to constantly have new people flowing into our lives and ministries. We lose objectivity and become defensive and territorial as the years go by. We don't always see the areas that need improvement.

> "We remember when days were lean and we finally got this organization on its feet. Let's not tamper with it."

> "It's been like this ever since I can remember. It's never been a problem. Let sleeping dogs lie."

> "When Mr. Forsythe founded this company, God rest his soul, he never intended for it to grow into the giant it is today. Yet we are able to keep that small family feeling. We simply must keep most things the way they were when he was here."

Creative people, while appreciating history, look at the present and strategize about the future. They see "effective" and aim for "more effective." They look at "holding our own" and push toward "we're leaders in our field." We do not only bend, break, or challenge rules because they don't work, but precisely because they could work better.

CHAPTER 11

Luke tells an interesting story:

Meanwhile a Jew named Apollos, a native of Alexandria, came to Ephesus. He was a learned man, with a thorough knowledge of the Scriptures. He had been instructed in the way of the Lord, and he spoke with great fervor and taught about Jesus accurately, though he knew only the baptism of John. He began to speak boldly in the synagogue. When Priscilla and Aquila heard him, they invited him to their home and explained to him the way of God more adequately. When Apollos wanted to go to Achaia, the brothers encouraged him and wrote to the disciples there to welcome him. On arriving, he was a great help to those who by grace had believed. For he vigorously refuted the Jews in public debate, proving from the Scriptures that Jesus was the Christ (Acts 18:24-28).

Apollos was not a bad preacher. On the contrary, he was eloquent and mighty in the scriptures. Most people who would hear such a preacher would say, "Leave him alone. He's doing just fine." But when Mr. and Mrs. Aquila heard him, they saw present effectiveness and future, greater effectiveness. Apollos already knew the way of God. Aquila and Priscilla wanted him to know and proclaim it more accurately.

We will never discover our most creative selves until we begin to exercise, regularly, a certain amount of dissatisfaction with things as they are. I don't mean that we take pessimism to every party and a sour outlook to every board meeting. I do mean that we must constantly be stretching, pushing, strategizing, and exploring the limits of our comfort zones. Some things are broke. Fix them! Some things ain't broke—fix them, too!

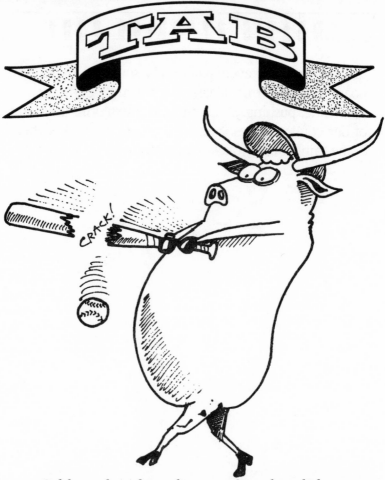

Celebrate three things that are right and good about your company, ministry, organization, or home. Write them out with some detail, perhaps a paragraph on each. Now look for an area in which each item could be improved. This will be painful; first, because you've probably described it in such positive detail that there does not seem to be room for improvement. Second, citing an area that could use improvement means you must get to work on it.

Proud of the fact that your family regularly has a devotional period together? Could it be less predictable? Could it be *more consistently held? Pleased that your company gives sub-stantial bonus checks to its employees at the end of the year? Could the company exhibit more concern for its employees throughout the year?*

We want to rock the boat! We want to upset the apple cart. We want to do whatever it takes to draw the best from ourselves and our situations.

❖

3. I don't know how long I'll be around.

This is usually the excuse of the person who thinks he/she is not only the most likely to be creative, but that he/she will be the only one. The reasoning goes something like this: "I'd better not stir up trouble, get things brewing, and get everybody excited, because when I leave there will be nobody to keep things going." This assumes two things, both false: first, that the creative changes made must last forever; second, that there are, or will be, no colleagues in creativity.

Leonard Haslim was NASA's 1988 inventor of the year. He sees what we all see, but looks at it differently. Having heard of an airliner crash caused by heavy ice on the wings which caused the plane to be too heavy for flight, Haslim set about to invent a wing de-icer. Using simple principles, such as "like charges repel," Haslim wrapped a sheet of rubber around a wing, putting elec-trical current carrying wires beneath the rubber. When power was applied, positive wires jumped away from positives and negatives away from negatives, busting the cakes of ice on top of them. How simple!

If a musician starts a bell choir in a church and then resigns three years later, there may be no qualified or interested parties to continue leading the ensemble. Does that mean it was not appreciated during its three year tenure? Not at all. Would it have been better for the musician not to have started the bell choir at all? Who knows if later down the road, another will revive the group?

Most of our ideas will not stand the test of time. They will not follow us for years to come. They will not be placed on our transcripts, resumes, or credit files. Our creative approaches and solutions will address a present problem, fill a void, meet a need. That is its own reward. The fact that we can't or won't commit the next twenty years of our lives to those problems is no reason to stand pat. Are you only going to attend our church for two years while in graduate school? Wonderful. What can you offer in two years that will help us now? Brevity in a place is not sufficient reason for lack of creative energy.

4. Ignorance.

The word ignorance has been given more bad press than it deserves. It literally means "without knowledge." It does not suggest that a person is not bright, is uncouth, or is uneducable. It simply means they are currently without knowledge in a particular area. Some are non-creative because, and only because, they do not know. They have not been exposed to models; they have not read the books; they have not heard the tapes. They do not know there is a more efficient, more stimulating, more motivating, more result-oriented way to accomplish their goals.

In most companies, churches, and organizations, a certain exposure to standard literature is assumed. You've certainly read that latest edition of *Leadership, Christianity Today, Moody Monthly, Reader's Digest,* the *New York Times,* the *Boston Globe, Forbes,* or *Inc.,* haven't you? Suppose you have not? You will not know what the others know. It's as simple as that. Much of the ability to "see," to be creative, presupposes at least a superficial working knowledge of the milieu in which you operate. The reason professional organizations exist is to keep individuals involved in a

given field, talking to each other and embracing common language and concerns.

Mission leaders in the local church need to know about the Association of Church Missions Committees.[1]

Musicians must avail themselves of the musicians' conferences held by denominations, colleges, conservatories of music, and conference centers.

Pastors should make it a point to attend a pastors' conference, institute of theology, or preaching workshop each year.

Executives should be attending management seminars at least annually.

Workshop-packed Christian education conferences would meet the needs of those in that field.

CHAPTER 11

Parents can take advantage of a number of family-life conferences such as those sponsored by Family Ministries of Campus Crusade for Christ.

Attendance at these functions is in addition to the discipline of personal growth. No conference or convention will stamp out ignorance if we are not committed to personal, aggressive development. In our society, we have to work hard to be ignorant! No person who deliberately embraces ignorance can simultaneously embrace creativity.

5. *There's a Messiah among us.*

Let's imagine a pastor by the name of Don Smickerson. He is the founding pastor of the Largo Street Community Church in Heartstown, U.S.A. As a young seminary grad, he came to this farming community in 1950. Starting with a home Bible study group, Pastor Smickerson watched his "baby" grow to become a vital church which now has a day school of 500 and a worshiping congregation of 3,100. Now in his sixty-fifth year, Smickerson has no plans to retire and is still quite capable and appreciated. Administratively, Smickerson insists that all decisions, great and small, come to his attention. In the name of "keeping abreast of what's going on," he stifles creativity. Most people whose ideas differ sharply from Pastor Smickerson's don't bother to submit proposals for new ministries. "*His* will be the only way things get done around here," said one under-utilized young man.

I plead with division managers, pastors, founding presidents, and leaders of all sorts—don't be so ever-present that you cripple your dreamers. If one thinks, at the outset, that his/her ideas will be rejected or shot down simply because they differ with yours, they will probably cease to share innovative thought. It is true, in matters of divine revelation, that

> Surely the Lord GOD does nothing unless He reveals His secret counsel to His servants the prophets (Amos 3:7, NASB).

But in matters of day-to-day operations and programming, God certainly does speak to ordinary people to whom he has given wonderful gifts. Leaders help create an atmosphere that either squashes or encourages ministry. Surely the leader must keep the organization on course, but we dare not do it at the risk of killing the spirit of the volunteer or salaried employee. The Messiah complex spells death for a ministry, company, or organization; not because the leader is ineffective, but because he thinks he *alone* is inspired.

Homer Egret started the Gainesville Lumber Company in 1947. The second world war was over and new housing construction was booming. As the business expanded, Homer found this "family of employees" doubling, tripling, and quadrupling in the first five years of business. Opening six lumber yards within the tri-state area, Homer found himself playing the part of a roving executive. As his sons, Craig and Dennis, joined the business, Homer turned some day-to-day operations over to them, but Homer was indisputably the chief executive officer. Visiting each yard weekly, he was always given great honor, respect, and deference. In the early 1980s Craig and Dennis proposed company-wide computerization that would enhance efficiency but would eliminate thirteen jobs in the billing department. Let's eavesdrop on a father-son conversation:

CRAIG: Pop, it's time we looked at consolidating our billing functions and record-keeping.

HOMER: That's always a good idea. We've gotta keep everything running smoothly.

DENNIS: One of the ways we've looked at doing this is by installing an efficient computer system.

HOMER: Everybody's getting into those things now. The old gas station down on Fifth and Collins just put in some fancy pumps with digital readings.

CRAIG: We can save $130,000 in the first year even after the purchase of equipment, according to the sales rep we consulted with.

HOMER: Our customers really like that personal touch our girls in billing give them.

DENNIS: Of course, we can customize our program so that we retain our famous personal touch.

HOMER: Glen's Plumbing went to computers and during a power outage he lost all his records when the computer got zapped. I don't trust them things.

CRAIG: They have very sophisticated ways to

prevent that from happening. We will have back-up power and copies of all records.

HOMER: They'll never replace humans, I tell ya. How are we going to learn all that stuff? It's just as fast to write it out by hand or run it through the typewriter. We still get our bills out within ten days and everything's in perfect order. Since 1947 we've been doing a great job. You haven't heard any complaints yet, have you?

DENNIS: No, Pop, but . . .

HOMER: Another thing: A lot of these fly-by-night operations won't be around when you have service problems. This computer thing is just a fad for some of them.

CRAIG: Certainly we'd go with a major company and . . .

HOMER: Now Peggy in accounts receivable—she's sixty-three and I remember when she came. It was three months after we opened. Ha! She did a little of everything in those days. She's stubborn. If you went to computers, she'd just up and quit.

DENNIS: We'd certainly structure the transitions so that adequate training . . .

HOMER: And I won't even mention Charlie in accounting. His green eyeshade would flip right off his head if he had to learn computers at this stage in the game. You know what they say

CHAPTER 11

about old dogs! Why don't we wait until some of the old-timers retire? Let the young folks do this computer stuff. I've spent the best part of my life building this company and I'm not going to hurt the ones who started with me in the early days. Just forget it.

CRAIG: But Pop . . .

HOMER: Trust me. This is not a good idea right now.

It may well be that Craig and Dennis will be able to persuade Homer to change his mind, but Homer is undoubtedly in charge. He remembers a day when the company could handle all billing by hand and when he knew every customer and employee by name. Craig and Dennis, with the help of an aggressive marketing consultant, have secured more contracts this year than in the previous three years and see the continual need for automation. As long as Homer is around, it will be assumed that he knows best. Even if he doesn't, who will argue with him? The company is his baby. He is the reason the employees, including Craig and Dennis, have jobs.

Switching contexts for a moment: Let's consider the hypothetical "Let's Open the Word of God" radio ministry that began in 1939. There was Brother John's favorite quartet that opened each broadcast with an Ira Sankey melody; a smooth-voiced announcer gave a word of welcome; Brother John came on with a lesson for the day; a closing appeal for financial support was made; and, with a cheerful "until next time," the closing music came in and faded.

WHAT'S STOPPING YOU?

We are now in the 1990s and not-so-subtle changes have taken place in broadcasting, Christian music, fund raising techniques/trends, audience profiles, and direct mail response. Brother John begins to make doctrinal purity an issue when the conversation turns to audience profiles. One has nothing to do with the other. Bright young communications majors interview for positions with the ministry but quickly realize that the "old man" is still back in 1939. New format proposals are quickly dismissed with a word about "avoiding modernism."

If you worked for Gainesville Lumber or the "Let's Open the Word of God" radio ministry, your creative juices would not flow as readily as they might elsewhere, because the "guru" in your midst would suppress your ideas. Often the best ideas of the innovators are dashed and destroyed because the person that could "give permission" to the dreamer, will not.

Many will respond to such a situation by leaving. Many others will simply not rock the boat and will wait until the old man dies. In the interim they don't bend, challenge, or break rules. They simply endure. Playing it safe, they hang on until the obstacle is removed. They anticipate the rejection of the guardian of the old way, who is usually the founder/savior of the organization, and do nothing that would suggest mutiny.

Where Do You Stand?

What's stopping you from being your most creative self? Fear? Insecurity? See any of these as the surmountables they are and handle them. The easiest phrase for you to utter is, "I can't be creative." Resist such a temptation!

CHAPTER 11

John Gardner, in his book *Excellence*, writes that there is an up and a down side to living in a democracy.

> Though our society surpasses others in rewarding "winners" without concern for their point of origin, it is also the form of society which gives less successful people the greatest ultimate control over the "winners."[2]

Essentially, Gardner says a society that grants privileges may also impose restrictions. The same society that allows the entrepreneur to gain wealth also enacts (via its electorate of rich and poor) laws that limit what that entrepreneur can do with his/her wealth. Gardner continues:

> This paradox creates one of the tensions which makes our society unique. There are impressive opportunities for the able individual to rise to the top. But those who do not rise are given

wide latitude in writing the rules which hem him in when he gets there.[3]

Let me apply this same tension to creativity. A refreshing aspect of our society is that we may dream large dreams, come up with wild ideas, and give vent to our most innovative selves.

But the same society that allows such creative freedom expects "safe," "responsible" behavior out of us. We are invited to "get crazy" and "act your age" at the same time. Often it is the non-innovative who call the shots for us. The tension is great and not to be overlooked. All the world's a circus for those of us who love to create. For others, life is a drag and we are an annoyance. Fellow creators, so much is at stake that we dare not let anyone "write the laws" for us.

Thomas B. Macaulay made a comment about genius that could easily apply to creativity. "[Genius] is subject to the same laws which regulate the production of cotton and molasses. The supply adjusts itself to the demand. The quantity may be diminished by restrictions, and multiplied by bounties."[4]

So may you, without excuse, be bountiful and not restricted!

Notes

1. ACMC, P. O. Box ACMC, Wheaton, Illinois, 60189-8000.

2. John Gardner, *Excellence* (New York: Harper & Row, 1961), 109.

3. Ibid., 110.

4. Thomas Macaulay, "On the Athenian Orators," (August 1824) *Macaulay's Complete Works*, XI (Green and Co., 1898), 340.

TALK TO YOURSELF

elax! This is not the part where I tell you to say, "I'm creative" and you shall be. No such promise will be coming from *my* pen. However, I do want to lead you in some creativity-affirming exercises that may help set a path for you to follow. One has said, "If you think you can or you can't, you're right." Constantly saying, "I'm not creative," "New ideas just don't come to me," "I haven't had a fresh thought in months," or "I can't think like that" only helps stifle rather than encourage your creativity. Every day, by what you say *to* and *about* yourself, you set yourself up for a generative life . . . or the lack of one.

I am cautious about these words, for much of what is written today is purely humanistic in that it suggests that "whatever the mind can conceive, man can achieve." Motivational books and tapes ask us to believe that if we repeat a phrase or ideology enough times we will achieve greatness. Citing some lines from the ancient book of Proverbs, "Eat thou not the bread of him that hath an evil eye, neither desire thou his dainty meats: For as he thinketh in his heart, so is he" (Proverbs 23:6-7a, KJV), writers have suggested that persons can possess whatever they can imagine. My friend, if you think you will become creative simply by saying so, think again. Nevertheless, you will enhance your creativity skills by transforming your self-perception.

When I was a youngster, probably in my tenth or eleventh year, my grandparents bought us a small plastic cartoon projector as a Christmas present. Bringing a couple of reels of black and white cartoons, Pop taught me how to thread the projector. He patiently demonstrated how to bend the film around the sprockets and thread it into the take-up reel. After one demonstration, Pop said, "Now you try it." I threaded the projector correctly and I will never forget his words: "I have the smartest grandson in the world!"

Years later, I asked Pop if he remembered that incident. He didn't, but I did! For all the years following that day until now, I have thought I was bright, skillful, teachable, quick to catch on. I would probably also have remembered if Pop had said, "I have the dumbest grandson in the world." And my life might have demonstrated my belief.

What memorable phrases are you depositing in your mind, to be trapped there for years to come? We are not simply talking about positive thinking here. We are talking about the stuff with which you program your mind. Action is always a part of that programming. If you would be creative, begin, now, to tell yourself that you are. Then do those things which foster creativity.

We have a way of deferring affirming words in favor of that which is safe. After all, if we don't say it, maybe we won't be held accountable for doing it. Perception and performance go together. Once you "see" yourself as a creative person, you must perform as one.

This differs from suggesting that you can generate creativity merely by saying so. Evangelical Christians are notorious for having perceptions of self not at all aligned with Scripture. "Greg, that was a beautiful solo you played this morning. You really know how to handle a flute." Greg then feels compelled to say, "Praise God," because if he were to say a simple "Thank you," it might imply that the talent was his and not God's. The giver of the compliment then feels as if he has not been spiritual enough, since he gave "praise" to the human actor (Greg) rather than to God. And so it goes. After a while, Greg no longer sees himself as one of God's primary players, but as a mere conduit as God plays the flute!

This is not at all what the Bible has in mind for us. When God created humanity, he did not do so with the idea that we would spend all our days groveling and denying the glory he placed in us.

Listen to the psalmist:

> When I consider your heavens, the work of your fingers, the moon and the stars, which you have set in place, what is man that you are

mindful of him, the son of man that you care for him? You made him a little lower than the heavenly beings and crowned him with glory and honor. You made him ruler over the works of your hands; you put everything under his feet: all flocks and herds, and the beasts of the field, the birds of the air, and the fish of the sea, all that swim the paths of the seas. O LORD our Lord, how majestic is your name in all the earth! (Psalm 8:3-9).

This is a far cry from how we often perceive ourselves. We react rather than reign. God has given us a key role in the earth. He takes no pleasure in our denying what he has designed.

Why are we not able to say, with confidence, "I am creative. After all, the God who brought all things out of nothing, created me and placed his glory in me"? You will never be as generative as you were designed to be until you begin to make those kinds of statements.

Let us get technically correct here. Only God creates *ex nihilo*. To bring something into existence *out of nothing* is to *exnihilate*. To pass something *into nothingness* from existence is to *annihilate*. Technically, we don't create *ex nihilo*. We take elements that already exist and rearrange them. We put those elements into forms in which they have not been seen. We are able to be creative because the creating and creative God of heaven and Scripture has been pleased to place some of his spark in us.

Saying you are creative does not mean that you

repeat some mystical mantra each day with the hope that repetition will breed competence. Rather, your self-perception as creative is a theological affirmation of the God who designed you for glory! Read Psalm 8 again. Do you see the splendor of humanity there? Have you gotten a glimpse of the greatness and creativity God has for you? See the same theme in the first book of the Bible:

> Then God said, "Let us make man in our image, in our likeness, and let them rule over the fish of the sea and the birds of the air, over the live-stock, over all the earth, and over all the crea-tures that move along the ground...." Now the LORD God had formed out of the ground all the beasts of the field and all the birds of the air. He brought them to the man to see what he would name them; and whatever the man called each living creature, that was its name. So the man gave names to all the livestock, the birds of the air and all the beasts of the field (Genesis 1:26; 2:19-20).

Does that sound like an invitation to say, "Oh no, please don't look at me. It is God who named the animals *through* me"? Don't misunderstand; I'm not advocating pride here. The truth is, any creativity we have, we have by the good gift of God. "What do you have that you did not receive?" Paul asks us in 1 Corinthians 4:7. But do allow me to argue for a perception of yourself out of which you say, "God has created me for glory." To say otherwise is to miss the point of creation and calling.

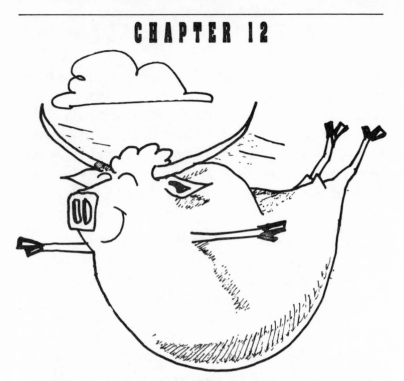

Theodore Roosevelt, twenty-sixth president of the United States, said, "Far better it is to dare mighty things, to win glorious triumphs even though checkered with failure, than to take rank with those poor saints who neither enjoy much nor suffer much, because they live in the gray twilight that knows not victory nor defeat."

What is the worst thing that could happen if you started seeing yourself as creative? What would be the results of your going around actually telling people you are creative? Some will celebrate with you. Others will wonder who died and left you boss. Still others will say that you only wish you were creative. They will be partially correct, but at least they will have been duly notified of your intended direction.

I have made a significant investment in motivational cassettes and books. Rare is the long drive on which I do not take some tapes that will help me improve my time management skills, help me overcome procrastination, or push me toward excellence. Most tapes lack the theological emphasis I would like, but they are valuable for what they set out to give the listener.

Do you know what happens to the mind after it is bombarded for two to three hours of affirming talk? It starts to believe it. If you drive at fifty-five miles an hour and drive twelve thousand miles a year, you are in your car more than two hundred hours. Think of how much you could feed into your mind in that amount of time. What you say to yourself about yourself is critical, if you are to be creative.

Thomas Edison, the prolific inventor who was committed to repetition and exploration, said, "If we did all the things we were capable of, we would literally astound ourselves." Just imagine what would happen if we began to say to ourselves everything we envisioned. What is the harm in saying it? It costs nothing and may open a door of much-needed confidence.

Now, my fellow creator, the next step is yours. Yours is the decision to live and work on the edge of excitement and innovation . . . or to seek the safe places. With your left brain telling you to take risks and throw away caution, you've got an exciting dilemma on your hands. Rudyard Kipling captured that dilemma well:

Much I owe to the lands that grew—
More to the Lives that fed—

But most to the Allah Who gave me
Two
Separate sides of my head.
Much I reflect on the Good and the True
In the faiths beneath the sun
But most upon Allah Who gave me
Two
Sides to my head, not one.
I would go without shirt or shoe,
Friend, tobacco or bread,
Sooner than lose for a minute the two
Separate sides of my head![1]

Tell yourself and others that you glory in your two-sided brain (created by Christ, by the way, contrary to Kipling!). And may you accomplish extraordinary feats through your creative decisions.

By now it is cliché, but let me tell you the story of the eaglet and the chicken. Always adventurous, a young boy wandered from his family's chicken farm and went climbing. He came upon an eagle's nest and, fascinated by it all, took an egg from the nest. When he arrived home, he placed the egg alongside some chicken eggs beneath a sitting hen. After hatching, the eagle looked and acted like the chicks . . . for awhile. As the eaglet grew it began to feel urges and promptings. It started wanting to do what chickens don't do. It wanted to fly, to climb, to soar. One day, it dared to try. The eaglet spread its wings and took to the sky.

After some years with chickens, it may be that we have managed to squash our desire to soar. But the urge and the prompting are still there. Consider this an invitation to soar with the eagles; to climb, to mount up, to put leagues between you and the earth beneath.

The alternative is to spend your days ground-bound, scratching in the dirt.

Note

1. Rudyard Kipling, *Rudyard Kipling's Verse* (London: Hodder & Stoughton, 1927).

he commitment to be creative never ends. Once you're in, you're in for life.

That sentence sounds so permanent, doesn't it? It suggests no turning back. Now, if you think I want you to say yes to creativity and never go back to an ordinary existence, you are absolutely correct! Having crossed the line from observer to being part of the team that makes things happen, there is no turning back.

I had a piano teacher who told me that she felt chained to that instrument. Having committed herself to its mastery and having invested innumerable hours and dollars in the pursuit, it was too late to do an about face. Now, if she did not practice, the piano seemed to call out to her, to demand her attention. She could not *not* practice. Ignoring the piano was no longer a possibility.

That's how I wish for you to see creative thinking. Having said yes, having taken the plunge, there is no going back for us. This journey into what can seem to be an abyss is nonetheless exhilarating. It may well separate you from your colleagues. Jesus reminded those who would follow him that if they did, it would mean separating from those with whom they were accustomed to spending time (Matthew 10:34-36; Luke 9:57-62). You gain a new set of colleagues when you follow the Christ.

Be not dismayed in your efforts to become generative, insightful, and fun, if some of your ground-bound chicken friends try to stop you. In fact, expect it and you will be that much ahead. This is terribly threatening for us! It threatens those who see their primary task as that of

EPILOGUE

protecting things as they were. Those curators of the past are certainly needed in many settings, but in others, they are a plain nuisance—and we, the creative, alarm them. But there is no turning back.

Because of your commitment to faith in Jesus Christ, make a commitment to creativity. Decide that you will not bore yourself all the way to the doors of death. Decide that you will live until you die. Jonathan Edwards, one of the most brilliant (and creative!) minds America ever produced, listed the following resolution as one of the thirteen which guided his life: "Resolved: That I shall live with all my might, while I do live."

It is critical that you start today, lest one of life's most important decisions be shelved. There never will be a more convenient time. There never will be a more fruitful time. There will never, ever, be a time when you are more ready or needy than you are right now.

Finally, know that becoming a truly creative person is a process. It does not happen overnight. You do not wake up one morning and discover, "I'm generative." You go along, depositing wonder-filled "stuff" into your mind, heart, and entire being. Before you know what has happened, you are seeing differently. You are hearing what others don't hear. You are reaching where others have not dared to put forth their hands and you are soaring high above the place to which you were once limited.

May it be said of you as was said of the climbers of one great peak. A reporter watched as they disappeared into the clouds and simply wrote, "When last seen, they were still climbing."

BIBLIOGRAPHY

Achtemeier, Elizabeth. *Creative Preaching: Finding the Words.* Nashville: Abingdon, 1980.

Adams, James L. *Conceptual Blockbusting: A Guide to Better Ideas.* New York: W. W. Norton & Company, 1974.

de Bono, Edward. *Lateral Thinking: Creativity Step by Step.* New York: Harper & Row, 1970.

_____. *New Think.* New York: Avon Books, 1967.

_____. *Six Thinking Hats.* Boston: Little, Brown and Company, 1985.

Edwards, Betty. *Drawing on the Right Side of the Brain.* Los Angeles: J. P. Tarcher, 1979.

Kagan, Jerome, ed. *The Act of Creation.* New York: Dell Publishing Co., Inc., 1964.

Lewis, David and Green, James. *Thinking Better.* New York: Rawson, Wade Publishers, 1982.

Nierenberg, Gerald I. *The Art of Creative Thinking.* New York: Simon & Schuster, Inc., 1982.

Nolan, Vincent. *The Innovator's Handbook.* New York: Viking Penguin Inc., 1987.

Nouwen, Henri. *Creative Ministry.* Garden City: Doubleday & Company, 1971.

Osborn, Alex F. *Applied Imagination: The Principles and Procedures of Creative Problem-Solving,* 3rd Revised Edition. New York: Charles Scribner's Sons, 1963.

Parnes, S. and Harding, H., eds. *A Source for Creative Thinking.* New York: Charles Scribner's Sons, 1962.

Torrance, E. Paul. *Creative Learning and Teaching.* New York: Dodd, Mead & Co., 1970.

Upton, Albert and Sampson, Richard W. *Creative Analysis.* New York: E. P. Dutton & Co., 1978.

Upton, Albert. *Design for Thinking.* Stanford: Stanford University Press, 1961.

von Oech, Roger. *A Whack on the Side of the Head.* New York: Warner Books, 1983.

_____. *A Kick in the Seat of the Pants.* New York: Harper & Row, 1986.

RESOURCES

Creative Think
Box 7354
Menlo Park, California 94026
(415) 321-6775

This organization, founded in 1977 by Roger von Oech, exists to stimulate creative thinking and innovation in business.

Nightingale-Conant
7300 North Lehigh Avenue
Chicago, Illinois 60648
(800) 323-3938

This is the largest producer of motivational audio and video cassettes in the world. Call and request their catalog.

Creative Education Foundation
1050 Union Road
Buffalo, New York 14224
(716) 675-3181

This organization does nothing but produce materials and sponsor workshops that teach creativity. They have a brochure of currently available materials that will make you drool. Not only do they publish the *Journal of Creative Behavior*, but they also produce the monthly newsletter, *Creativity in Action*, fondly dubbed CIA. Call them for a packet of information.